SILVER

FROM THE LAND OF ISRAEL

A New Light on the
Sabbath and Holidays

We must value the true measure of lights of holiness, which sparkle at a particular point, according to their hidden diffusion throughout the entire plane. They travel in secret paths and concealed currents, until they are revealed in that illuminating point.

Holiness in time is distributed across the entire continuum of time – "Blessed be the Eternal, each day" (Ps. 68:20). Light-waves of holiness travel and are drawn in a hidden fashion, until they are expressed and revealed in [particular] moments of holiness, in the holiness of Shabbat ... and the holiness of the holidays.

(Orot HaKodesh vol. II, p. 303)

"Ramah and the Tomb of Rachel" from *The Biblical Keepsake* (London, 1835), p. 49

SILVER

FROM THE LAND OF ISRAEL

A new light on the
Sabbath and Holidays
from the writings of

Rabbi Abraham Isaac HaKohen Kook

✴

Rabbi Chanan Morrison

URIM PUBLICATIONS
Jerusalem ◆ New York

Silver From the Land of Israel: A New Light on the Sabbath and Holidays From
the Writings of Rabbi Abraham Isaac HaKohen Kook
by Rabbi Chanan Morrison

First Edition. Printed in Israel.
ISBN: 978-965-524-042-9
Book design and typesetting by Ariel Walden, Bookraft

Urim Publications, PO Box 52287, Jerusalem 91521 Israel

Lambda Publishers Inc.
3709 13th Avenue Brooklyn, New York 11218 USA
Tel: 718-972-5449 Fax: 718-972-6307, urim_pub@netvision.net.il

www.UrimPublications.com

WE DEDICATE THIS volume of Rabbi Kook's many illuminating and novel essays on the Sabbath and Holidays in loving memory of our parents

MARJORIE and SHIMON SUMNER

Shimon was a brilliant student who was in the first Smicha class ordained by Rav Yitzchok Hutner, *zt"l*, of the Yeshiva Rabbi Chaim Berlin. After serving as a principal in Saint Paul, Minnesota, Shimon and his bride Margie returned to New York where he established a retail and service business. His employees were treated like family and his family was treated like royalty. Shimmy had the broadest smile, a playful sense of humor and the lightest heart. He danced, he learned, he bubbled, he repaired, he chauffeured, he cooked, he studied and he met every challenge with warmth and devotion. Shimon's philanthropy not only involved donations to major institutions, but he also filled every extended hand.

Margie was a most engaging woman. Every shopkeeper, mechanic, neighbor and professional were not casual acquaintances, but friends. She remembered each of their names and whatever slice of their life they shared with her. Margie made everyone feel cherished and important. A great raconteur who absorbed every detail, she could regale you for hours, but it would only feel like minutes. Always giving gifts, never missing an opportunity to say thank you, Margie was a true "mentch."

Their daughter was their life, their son-in-law was their prince, their grandchildren were their world. Margie never had a harsh word with her sister. With unparalleled devotion to family, an open hand and an open mind, they always said "yes, we can." Margie and Shimon blessed us with fierce love, unwavering protection and sparkling memories. Shabbos and Yom Tov were always treasured and our parents would have been proud to have been associated with this insightful scholarship.

REVA and MARTY OLINER
Lawrence, NY

Dedicated to my first five "books" – Segulah, Hemda, Temima, Shalva Esther, and Zimra.

May they be inscribed for "a wealth and length of days, to contemplate Your Torah and perform its mitzvot, blessed with wisdom and insight to understand the depths of its inner secrets."

CONTENTS

CONTENTS

CONTENTS

CONTENTS

Preface

THE SUDDEN OUTBREAK of World War I found Rabbi Abraham Isaac Kook in Germany, where he had traveled to attend an important rabbinical conference. Trapped in Europe, he spent the war years outside of Israel – first in Switzerland, and then in England, where he served as rabbi of the prestigious Machzikei HaDat synagogue. Rav Kook[1] accepted the London position on condition that he would be free to leave as soon as it would be possible to return to *Eretz Yisrael*.

Several days before the Passover holiday, the rabbi penned a short letter to his son Tzvi Yehudah. He apologized for its brevity – he had just arrived in London, after spending several difficult weeks in England without proper lodgings. In addition to the endless arrangements due to the move and settling in as the new rabbi of the community, he was busy preparing for the Passover holiday and answering numerous Halachic queries from his congregants. Continual disturbances kept him away what he truly loved – reflecting and writing on philosophical-spiritual matters.

---

1   In this book, "Rav Kook" always refers to Rabbi Abraham Isaac HaKohen Kook (1865–1935), the first chief rabbi of pre-state Israel. For an account of his life, see *An Angel Among Men* by Rabbi Simcha Raz, translated by Rabbi Moshe Lichtman (Jerusalem: Kol Mevaser, 2003).

Nonetheless, Rav Kook found time to record a few lines about Passover's unique quality of freedom. Of special interest are his remarks concerning the concept of holiness in time. The special sanctity of the Sabbath, he wrote, is not restricted to the twenty-four hours of the Sabbath day. Rather, its holy influence spreads throughout the week. When do we fulfill the Torah's command to "Remember the Sabbath day to sanctify it" (Ex. 20:7)? According to the *Mechilta*, this mitzvah is not on the Sabbath itself but during the week – each day we should remember and prepare for the Sabbath. The Sabbath is thus a source of blessing for the entire week. But what is the mechanism for this dissemination of holiness?

ঌ THE INNKEEPER'S PRAYERS

To help clarify Rav Kook's idea, I will briefly repeat a well-known Chassidic tale. It is said that the Baal Shem Tov[2] once lodged in the inn of an unlearned Jew who lived in the middle of a forest. When the rabbi rose early in the morning to recite his morning prayers, he saw the innkeeper join him. A holy *tzaddik*, the Baal Shem Tov would recite each word of prayer slowly and carefully, with profound *kavanot*. When he finished his prayers, he was amazed to find that the innkeeper was still praying. This simple Jew had not exhibited any other signs of exceptional piety, and the Baal Shem Tov was curious why his prayers were so lengthy.

It turned out the innkeeper was so unlettered that he was unable to decipher the instructions in the prayer book. Thus every morning he would read the prayer book from cover to cover – reciting the morning, afternoon, and evening prayers, prayers for the weekday, for the Sabbath, for the holidays – everything. The Baal Shem Tov offered to help the man, and instructed him to place bits of paper to mark the different prayers.

The innkeeper was delighted with this arrangement, but his joy was short-lived. The following day a terrific wind came and scattered all of the little markers. The man rushed to the Baal Shem Tov, entreating him to place new markers in his prayer book. But this time the *tzaddik* refused. The Baal

2 Rabbi Israel ben Eliezer (1698–1760), founder of the Hasidic movement.

Shem Tov realized that the wind was a sign from heaven. The innkeeper's unusual prayers were highly valued just the way they were – from the beginning to the end of the *siddur*.

The point of this story is clear. We live in a time-bound reality, with fixed times for particular prayers and holidays. On Passover we celebrate our freedom, on Shavuot we rejoice in the Torah, on Yom Kippur we repent, and so on. But on a deeper and truer level, the themes of these different prayers and holidays are relevant at all times, every day of the year. The innkeeper's prayers belonged to a higher realm, a realm beyond the limitations of time.

❧ SANCTITY IN TIME

Now we may understand how the holiness of the Sabbath disseminates to the rest of the week. It is not, Rav Kook explained, that the Sabbath influences the rest of the week. Rather, this special holiness is *always* present, albeit hidden under the surface.

> The overall concept concerning the diffusion of noble feelings of holiness outside of their specific time, such as the continuation of the holiness of the Sabbath to the days of the week, must be based on the inner recognition that elevated holiness is secreted in all things. Divine ideals exist fully in every point and aspect, in life, time, and place . . . . The appearance of secularity is but a mask, concealing all of the radiant light of desired and beloved life. [The hidden holiness] emanates from God's pleasantness and enters the entirety of worlds, the entirety of souls, and the entirety of our inner lives.
>
> Holiness comes at set times and removes the scarf, stripping away the cloak that conceals. And the holy light with all of its beloved traits is revealed, warming our hearts with pleasantness of its contemplations, satiating us with the joy of its pleasures. We take delight in God and His goodness, and our hearts are filled with a sublime pleasure. (*Igrot HaRe'iyah* vol. III, p. 35)

These observations are complemented by an essay in *Orot HaKodesh* (vol. II, p. 303), which describes the phenomenon of "holy lights which sparkle in a particular point." To properly value the true measure of these holy lights, we must recognize that they are in fact diffused throughout the entire plane, but in a hidden fashion. They lie in concealed lines "until they are revealed in that illuminated point."

In a fashion typical of Rav Kook, he then applied this concept to several realms. One may find this phenomenon in the realm of the *soul*: all souls contain a latent holiness, but this potential is fully revealed in the Jewish soul. It similarly occurs in the dimension of *space*: holiness fills the entire universe, but is revealed in the land of Israel and to a greater extent in Jerusalem and the holy Temple. And, as discussed above, it occurs in the dimension of *time*; Divine blessings reside in each day, but they are revealed in special times, the Sabbath and the holidays.

To help explain this phenomenon, Rav Kook used an example from the human body. Why is it that we see with our eyes and hear with our ears?

Our ability to perceive the outside world comes from our overall life-force. Every cell in the body contains the genetic code for sensory organs. Thus the entire body has the potential to see and hear. But this potential is only revealed in those organs most qualified for these specific functions. It is only the eye that sees and the ear that hears, even though these sensory capabilities exist equally throughout the body. So, too, various aspects of holiness exist uniformly over time; but their potential is realized and revealed in special times during the year.

◆ ◆ ◆

After the warm reception of my first book of essays on Rav Kook's thought, *Gold from the Land of Israel* (Jerusalem: Urim Publications, 2006), several acquaintances suggested that a complementary volume was needed. *Gold* organizes Rav Kook's writings according to the weekly Torah reading, thus providing a valuable resource for the Shabbat table. But what about the holidays? Thus was born this volume.[3]

While reviews of *Gold from the Land of Israel* were very positive, one

---

3   While the vast majority of essays in this book are new, I have taken the liberty of reprinting

reviewer raised an issue I think worthwhile addressing. He expressed concern that a book of essays collected from various writings of Rav Kook, without developing those ideas and organizing them topically, will fail to provide to the reader a sense of their overall context.

The truth is that any sense of order in Rav Kook's writings is for the most part artificial. Rav Kook penned the vast majority of his non-Halachic books in the form of short, inspired passages that he recorded in notebooks. As Rav Kook testified about himself, "I write according to *havrakot* [bursts of inspired thought]" (*Shivchei HaRe'iyah*, p. 292). These passages were later organized into topics and chapters and books by his disciples, primarily Rabbi David Cohen and his son Rabbi Tzvi Yehuda Kook. The few attempts that Rav Kook himself made at organizing his thought into a systematic work, such as the beginning chapters of *Orot HaTeshuvah* and *Olat Re'iyah*, were abandoned at some point, only to be completed by his son. In general, Rav Kook left the organization to others. Thus we read Rabbi Cohen's account of how he came to be the editor of *Orot HaKodesh*:

> One day I approached [Rav Kook] with a question. "Our master, you have holiness, spirit, a unique influence. But does the Rav also have a *Torah* – a systematic instructional content, a methodology?"
>
> And the answer – "Yes, certainly."
>
> From that moment, I decided to clarify the Rav's Torah as a complete Divine methodology, with its categories and fundamental principles. And then, according to these categories, I selected from his writings and arranged them into articles. (*Orot HaKodesh* vol. I, p. 18)

---

a few articles that appeared in *Gold from the Land of Israel* and deal directly with the holidays.

I must acknowledge the invaluable influence of Rabbi Pesach Jaffe's *Celebration of the Soul* (Genesis Jerusalem Press, 1992), an excellent translation of Rabbi Moshe Zvi Neriah's book on the holidays, *Mo'adei HaRe'iyah*. Pesach ל"ז was a fellow student at the Mercaz HaRav yeshiva and a close personal friend. His untimely passing served as a wake-up call to me to "let your wellsprings spread forth," and carry on the work of disseminating Rav Kook's teachings in English.

As Rabbi Cohen testified, there *is* a system and methodology in Rav Kook's thought. Yet the presentation of his thought as a methodical and ordered system is not a natural feature of Rav Kook's own writings, but the product of the intellectual efforts of his students and disciples.

Another attempt to organize Rav Kook's thought took place in 1936, one year after Rav Kook's passing. Rabbi Moshe Zvi Neriah called his short treatise *Mishnat HaRav* – a name that alludes to earlier attempts to systematize Torah into a methodical structure, such as Rabbi Yehuda HaNasi's Mishnah and Maimonides' *Mishneh Torah*. In a beautifully written preface, Rabbi Neriah reflected that these efforts to organize, while necessary, do not indicate a higher level of Torah wisdom. On the contrary, the very need to classify and order is a sign of spiritual decline:

> When did Judaism begin to organize its teachings? When its body became shriveled and his soul flew away. As long as the nation's body was fresh, spiritual life flowed in it in all its strength. The spirit of prophecy pounded in vigor. There was no need to demarcate life's boundaries, to define their perimeters. They found their path naturally.
>
> But when prophecy ceased and the spring of spiritual flow stopped, Judaism's soul needed to be contained within the pure vessels of Torah-fences; and the World to Come is only promised to those who study *Halachot* each day. The soul was hidden away in the Mishnah.[4]
>
> We learned this teaching in our master's *Beit Midrash*. And now we apply it to his own Torah.
>
> The Rav was a high priest "to the Most High God." His world was his temple; his life was his spiritual work. His thought and his soul blended together in one single entity. His life of holiness was a continuation of

---

4   The Oral Law was not meant to be written down (*Gittin* 60b). Rabbi Yehudah HaNasi relaxed this prohibition when he compiled the Mishnah in the second century, due to concern that the Torah's integrity would be compromised in the impending exile and dispersion.

his teachings; and his teachings were a limited revelation of his inner life-content.

All of his words were like coals of fire, and he himself was a holy flame. Those close to him were drawn by the radiance of his light and overwhelmed in the sea of his thought. Due to his profound awareness of powerful inner unity, of the universality of Torah and the world, the infinite Light of "God is one and His Name is one," transcendent and immanent in all worlds – he could not confine his words and set them down in an ordered and summarized fashion. They burst forth and surged with a great rush, as much as his holy mouth was able to articulate, as much as his pen was able to race across the page . . .

There is no chronological order in our master's Torah, no structure to his teachings. His words were not polished and edited. The editor's hand never touched them. They stand before us in their pristine splendor, as when they first appeared – true, authentic articulations of the soul, like the very essence of holy life. The Rav himself did not edit his writing, for he knew that the words did not appear arbitrarily, but flowed from the very depths. . . .

During his lifetime, all of the sparks were united in his great fire; all of the streams flowed to the ocean. But now after his passing, all of the sparks need to be brought together, to be united as a torch, so that its flame will rise on its own accord. In their current state, they appear only as separate, distinct details. They demand to be included in the "realm of unity" – that realm that our master was so much a part of.

While it is important to "unite the sparks" of Rav Kook's Torah into a logical, structured methodology, there is something artificial and even heartless in this act of dissecting and classifying a living Torah. Clearly there were basic principles and axioms that influenced how Rav Kook looked at all things, in the Torah and in the world; but these were part and parcel with his life. "His life of holiness was a continuation of his teachings; and his teachings were a limited revelation of his inner life-content."

What is common to all of Rav Kook's writings is a fundamental outlook, a God-centric worldview that everything has its place and purpose. Our task is to uncover the world's underlying unity and harmony. Such an all-inclusive approach fears nothing. Even the purest of evil, as represented by Amalek and an ideology diametrically opposed to the ethical-spiritual mission of Israel, only needs to be obliterated "under the heavens" (Deut. 25:19). But "above the heavens" – beyond the normative boundaries of good and evil – even Amalek has a place (*Mussar Avicha, Middot HaRe'iyah, Ahavah*).

In this work, as in *Gold from the Land of Israel*, I have tried to navigate a fine path, aiming to elucidate Rav Kook's ideas without expanding them to directions not found in the original. It is my hope that these essays remain faithful to the spirit of the original Hebrew writings, even if they are not a direct translation of Rav Kook's words. If I succeed in inspiring the reader to go back and study the original texts, then my efforts have been worthwhile.

As with any book, a few acknowledgments are in order. I wish to extend sincere thanks to my publisher, Tzvi Mauer of Urim Publications, for his support and encouragement, with this book as well as its predecessor; to my editor, Sara Rosenbaum, whose keen eye caught many errors and inconsistencies, and whose persistent probing forced me to clarify my thoughts and presentation; to my family and especially my wife, Gaila, for good-natured acceptance of the countless hours spent preparing this book. And finally, to the One "Who gave us the Torah of truth and implanted within us eternal life" – for the privilege and honor of studying אולפן חדתא מבחירי צדיקיא, this renewed Torah, fresh and vibrant, "from the springs of redemption" (Isaiah 12:3).

"Please make the words of Your Torah be pleasant in our mouths . . . so that we and our descendants, and the descendants of Your people Israel, will all know Your Name and study Your Torah for its own sake."

— CHANAN MORRISON
Av 5770 /July 2010
Mitzpe Yericho, Israel
http://ravkooktorah.org

Common Abbreviations

Gen. – Genesis
Ex. – Exodus
Lev. – Leviticus
Num. – Numbers
Deut. – Deuteronomy
Ps. – Psalms
Ecc. – Ecclesiastes

THE SABBATH
שבת

Freeing the Soul

Every Sabbath we shed the trappings of mundane life. "With the Sabbath comes rest."[1] The soul begins to free itself of its heavy shackles. It seeks higher paths, spiritual acquisitions befitting its true nature.

(Introduction to *Shabbat Ha'Aretz*, p. 8)

1 Rashi on Gen. 2:2, based on *Breishit Rabbah* 10:9.

Sabbath Peace, Inside and Out[1]

✣ CHECKING POCKETS

Sometimes it is the seemingly insignificant details that enable us to see the big picture.

> Hanania taught: One should examine one's garments on Sabbath eve before nightfall. Rav Yosef observed: This is a great law for the Sabbath.
>
> (*Shabbat* 12a)

The Sages sought to prevent one from unknowingly carrying objects in the public domain on Shabbat. This is perhaps a useful suggestion, but what makes it such an important principle – "a great law for the Sabbath"? After all, even if one were to accidently carry an object forgotten in one's pocket, this would fall under the Halachic category of *mitaseik* – an unintentional act for which one is not at all culpable. Why did Rav Yosef so highly praise Hanania's advice? Is checking one's pockets really so central to Sabbath observance?

---

1   Adapted from *Olat Re'iyah* vol. II, p. 28; *Ein Ayah* vol. III on *Shabbat* 12a (1:42).

ঌ SABBATH HARMONY

We live out our lives in two realms. There is our inner world – our ideals and moral principles, our aspirations and spiritual goals. And there is our outer world – our actions in the "real" world, our struggles to eke out a living and tend to our physical needs in a challenging and competitive world. The greater the dissonance between our inner and outer lives, between our elevated ideals and our day-to-day actions, the further we will have strayed from our Divine image and true inner self.

Shabbat, however, provides an opportunity to attain a degree of harmony between our inner and outer lives.

The holiness and tranquility of Shabbat help enrich our inner lives. Shabbat is a state that is very different from our workday lives, which have been complicated and even compromised by life's myriad calculations and moral struggles. "God made man straight, but they sought many intrigues" (Ecc. 7:29).

The Sabbath, with its elevated holiness, comes to restore the purity of inner life that was suppressed and eroded by the corrupting influences of day-to-day life, influences that often contradict our true values and goals. But the power of Sabbath peace is even greater. Not only does Shabbat restore our inner world, but it reaches out to our outer world. The spiritual rest of Shabbat enables our outer life to be in harmony with our inner life, bestowing it a spirit of peace and holiness, joy and grace.

ঌ GREAT PRINCIPLE OF SHABBAT

Now we may begin to understand the importance that the Sages placed on observing the Sabbath, even in life's external aspects. The Hebrew word for clothing, *beged*, comes from the root *bagad*, meaning "to betray"; for clothes can hide and betray the true inner self. On Shabbat, however, even the most superficial facets of our lives, our clothes and pockets, should reflect the sanctity of the Sabbath day.

The Sages prohibited certain activities because of *marit ayin*, an action's superficial appearance as inappropriate for Shabbat. And we are commanded to wear special clothing in honor of the Sabbath (*Shabbat* 113a). These external displays of Sabbath holiness are meant to ensure that its spirit of peace and harmony will permeate and refine our outer lives.

For this reason we should be careful even in situations that do not truly desecrate the Sabbath. Since they can occur frequently, they have the potential to dilute its sanctity. Forgetting an object in one's pocket does not truly entail Sabbath desecration; it is a completely mindless and unintentional act (Tosafot on *Shabbat* 11a). But the realm of external actions does not make these fine distinctions between degrees of intention. On the superficial, physical plane, some measure of desecration of Sabbath peace has taken place.

Rav Yosef praised this advice to check one's pockets before Shabbat as "a great law for the Sabbath." He recognized that this *halachah* fulfills the ideal of Shabbat as a force of holiness binding together the spiritual heights of our inner self together with the most superficial aspects of our physical existence. This is truly a great principle, refining the sanctity of the Sabbath and guarding its character, as it seeks to balance our inner and outer worlds, our highest aspirations with our day-to-day actions and external aspects of life.

The Proper Time to Light[1]

IT IS CUSTOMARY in most Jewish communities to light Sabbath candles 18 minutes before sundown. The Talmud (*Shabbat* 23b) records a conversation between fifth-century scholar Rav Yosef and his wife regarding the proper time to light.

⅍ NOT TOO EARLY, NOT TOO LATE

When Rav Yosef saw his wife lighting just moments before sundown, he gently rebuked her, explaining that the candles should be lit earlier, while it is still light outside. He compared the Sabbath lights to the pillar of fire that led the Israelites during their travels in the desert.

> The Torah states: "The cloud-pillar by day and the fire-pillar by night never left their place in front of the people" (Ex. 13:22). This teaches that the cloud-pillar would complete the task of the fire-pillar, and visa-versa.

In other words, the cloud-pillar would appear shortly before the start of day, and the fire-pillar would appear shortly before the night. So too, we should light Sabbath candles before the start of night.

---

1   Adapted from *Ein Ayah* vol. III on *Shabbat* 23b (2:31).

Upon hearing this, Rav Yosef's wife considered lighting much earlier Friday afternoon. But the scholar instructed her to light "not too early and not too late."

This account requires clarification. What is the connection between pillars of fire and Sabbath candles? And why should one light not too early and not too late?

✒ FIRE AND CLOUD

The pillars of fire and cloud provided a visual focus for the Israelites in their travels across the vast desert. At first glance, it would seem that these two phenomena were unrelated, since they served opposite functions. The fire-pillar lit up the night, while the cloud-pillar blocked the desert sun and provided shade. But in fact, they shared a common purpose, as they both provided a continual point of reference for the people. As Rav Yosef taught, each one completed the work of the other. This complementary relationship expressed itself in the fact that, as the day waned, the fire-pillar already began to appear. And as the night neared its end, the cloud-pillar would become visible.

Similarly, Sabbath lights are a focal point of the Sabbath's inner peace and holiness. Like the pillars of fire and cloud, we have two opposites – the Sabbath and the days of week. And like the pillars, they also share an inner connection. The enlightenment of Shabbat should not be confined to the twenty-four hours of the Sabbath day, but should influence and benefit the entire week. By lighting the Sabbath candles before Shabbat has commenced, we demonstrate that the Sabbath light casts its spiritual radiance over the other days of the week.

However, lighting too early is also inappropriate. The weekdays have their own function and purpose. Without the six days of activity, we could not fully experience and appreciate the spiritual rest of Shabbat. Just as a white piece of paper stands out more clearly when contrasted against a black background, so, too, the holiness of the Sabbath is more vivid against the background of six days of work.

‰ EXILE AND REDEMPTION

The final redemption is described as a time that is "completely Sabbath" (*Tamid* 33b). The redemption also has its polar opposite – the period of exile. Yet each is required in its own time. Were the redemption to come before its time, we would be unprepared for it, and blinded by its brilliant light. As Rav Yosef taught, the light needs to come at the proper time. Not too early, not too late.

The Sabbath Bride[1]

THE FRIDAY EVENING liturgical song *Lechah Dodi*[2] compares the Sabbath to a bride: לְכָה דוֹדִי לִקְרַאת כַּלָּה, פְּנֵי שַׁבָּת נְקַבְּלָה – "Come my friend, toward the bride; let us greet the Sabbath." What does this metaphor teach us?

๑ A TASTE OF THE WORLD TO COME

The Sabbath is a time of closeness to Torah and spiritual enlightenment. Through the light of our *neshamah yeteirah*, our special "Sabbath soul," we are able to grasp that which was distant and concealed from us during the weekdays.

This special receptiveness to Torah on the Sabbath is similar to the feelings of a bride toward her new husband. The bride does not know her husband in a deep, intimate way, the way a wife married for many years does. Yet there is an excitement and tremendous joy in the bride's love, which stems from the newness of the relationship.

The Talmud in *Berachot* 57b teaches that the Sabbath is a "taste of the World to Come." One day a week we can "taste" some of the holiness and

---

1 Adapted from *Olat Re'iyah* vol. II, p. 21.
2 Composed by 16th-century Kabbalist Rabbi Shlomo Alkabetz of Safed.

knowledge that will fill the world in the future era, a time of pure and continual Sabbath.

Our weekly Sabbath does not have the depth of enlightenment that will grace the World to Come, but there is a delight of newness, like the excitement and elation of a young bride. This bridal joy is particularly appropriate at the very start of the Sabbath, as we celebrate to greet her with *Lecha Dodi*.

The future world will also be blessed with a newlywed joy, as it says, "God will rejoice over you as a groom rejoices over his bride." This joy will be the product of an enlightenment that grows continually brighter, as the souls in the World to Come rejoice in their constant renewal and elevation.

Shabbat and Water[1]

҉ THE SABBATH *AMIDAH* PRAYER

Unlike the weekday *Amidah* ("standing prayer") that contains nineteen blessings, the Sabbath *Amidah* only has seven blessings. Why seven? The Talmud (*Berachot* 29a) explains that these seven blessings correspond to the seven times the phrase "God's voice" appears in Psalm 29.

> God's voice is upon the waters.
> God's voice is in strength.
> God's voice is in beauty.
> God's voice shatters the cedars.
> God's voice hews with flames of fire.
> God's voice makes the desert tremble.
> God's voice frightens the deer and strips the forest bare.

Why did the Sages associate this psalm, which contains not a single mention of Shabbat, to the Sabbath prayers? Also, why did they describe this psalm as the one that David composed "upon the waters"? Why the emphasis on water?

---

1   Adapted from *Olat Re'iyah* vol. II, pp. 19–20; *Ein Ayah* vol. I on *Berachot* 29a (4:43).

31

﹌ WATERS OF DESTRUCTION

The world appears most advanced and perfected when seen in its developed, built-up state. But upon deeper reflection, it is possible to recognize that there is also a need for destructive forces in the world. If we can perceive the benefits of destructive phenomena – like the positive role played by forest fires in the growth and regeneration of a forest – then we may grasp how also these forces indicate the underlying purpose and Divine wisdom governing the universe.

Water is a particularly apt metaphor for nature's destructive forces. Water, the seas and the oceans, are the antithesis of human progress and civilization. David composed Psalm 29 while reflecting "upon the water." He contemplated the great destructive forces in the world – leaving mighty cedars shattered, deserts shaking, and forests stripped bare – and in their deafening roar of upheaval he was able to hear the voice of God. Thus the phrase "God's voice" is the psalm's leitmotif, repeated seven times.

This insight is most clearly revealed in the spectacular devastation of cultivated land by floodwaters in the time of Noah. Thus the psalm concludes by recalling the tremendous destruction of the Flood – "God sat enthroned at the Flood" (29:10) – a destruction that cleansed the world of all that was irretrievably evil.

﹌ SABBATH REST

What does all this have to do with the Sabbath? We mistakenly think that our greatest achievements are to be found in our actions and practical accomplishments. Idleness and inactivity are assumed to be inconsequential, if not negative, aspects of life.

In truth, it is *rest* that perfects all actions. Rest is a contemplative process that gives meaning and purpose to our endeavors. This is the value of *menuchah*, the spiritual rest on the Sabbath day. It deepens our intellectual awareness and enhances our spiritual life. The Sabbath rest crowns our weekday activities, directing them toward their true purpose.

✦ SEVEN BLESSINGS

Now we may understand why the Sabbath *Amidah* prayer contains seven blessings. The number seven incorporates six – corresponding to the six days of creative activity – plus an additional seventh dimension of direction and purpose.[2] The seven blessings of the Sabbath *Amidah* teach that the *menuchah* of Shabbat is not just a negative quality, a cessation from productive work, but rather the development of our moral faculties and spiritual direction, cultivating our closeness to God and His ways.

---

2   Cf. *Tiferet Yisrael* ch. 40, where the Maharal (Rabbi Yehudah Loew of Prague, 1525–1609) explains the significance of the number seven as the physical universe – represented by the six sides of a three-dimensional box – plus one, its inner direction or content.

What is True Success?[1]

It is customary on Friday night to read the Mishnah בַּמֶּה מַדְלִיקִין, the second chapter of tractate *Shabbat*. This Mishnah enumerates those oils unsuitable for Sabbath lights as they are not drawn to the wick and do not light well. The Talmud (*Shabbat* 21a) records a discussion regarding the identity of one of these ineligible oils – *keek* oil.

> Samuel said: I asked all of the seafarers, and they told me that there is a certain bird in the faraway towns overseas called a *keek*.
>
> Rabbi Isaac said: It is cottonseed oil.
>
> [Rabbi Shimon ben] Lakish said: It is oil from Jonah's *kikayon* plant.

According to Rav Kook, these three scholars were not just attempting to determine the identity of some obscure oil. Rather, they were discussing a far more significant question: What is the source of true happiness and success in life? This topic is integrally connected to the Sabbath since it is a day of introspection, a time when we are able to take a break from life's hectic pace

---

1   Adapted from *Ein Ayah* vol. III on *Shabbat* 21a (2:1).

and examine our lives and our goals. The Sabbath candles in particular are a metaphor for spiritual illumination and *shalom bayit*, inner peace.

The various oils used to feed the lights symbolize different forms of wealth and success. Some oils burn more smoothly and produce a brighter light than others; so, too, some types of success generate greater inner joy and satisfaction. The Mishnah, then, is teaching us which goals are truly worthwhile – what is real success.

✸ THREE INDICATORS OF FALSE SUCCESS

The basic rule of the Mishnah is that oils that do not light well, oils that are not "drawn to the wick," are disqualified. In other words, goals which do not match the inner soul will not truly fulfill our needs and rejoice our spirits. Real success must be "drawn to the wick" – it must be integrally related to the soul and its spiritual goals.

The three explanations of *keek* oil, an oil inappropriate for the Sabbath, correspond to three types of artificial success. Samuel spoke of overseas towns in distant locales, far away from centers of Torah study and well-established Jewish communities. These places are destinations for merchants pursuing wealth and riches. And sailors, whom Samuel queried, are typically individuals with low moral standards. Thus the *keek* bird of the faraway towns represents those who chase after money and profits, at the expense of family and communal life, as well as their own ethical standards. This is the first false goal that should be rejected.

The second false goal is not wealth itself, but the lavish lifestyle and other material pleasures that it can buy. According to Rabbi Isaac, *keek* is cottonseed oil. Grapes and their primary product, wine, are a symbol of joy; we inaugurate festive occasions with a glass of wine. Cotton, on the other hand, is a metaphor for superficial happiness. The leaves of the cotton plant are similar to those of a grape-vine, and in Hebrew, cotton is called *tzemer gefen* – literally, "grape-wool." Like the grape, the cotton plant provides us with a very important product. However, the use of cotton is strictly external, producing clothing to cover the body. Unlike true grapes, this "cotton" joy does not touch the soul and cannot truly warm the heart. So, too, a person who spends his life pursuing material pleasures will discover that, despite his efforts, he fails to attain true, inner happiness.

Rabbi Shimon ben Lakish spoke of Jonah's *kikayon* plant, indicating a fundamental aspect which helps us distinguish between true and false success. What was the outstanding characteristic of the *kikayon*? Its fleeting existence – "in one night it appeared and in one night it was gone" (Jonah 4:10). Short-lived pleasures and quickly forgotten diversions are not suitable for the inner joy and light as represented by the Sabbath candles. Enduring happiness may only be attained through sincere efforts in spiritual pursuits, in Torah study and acts of kindness.

The Sabbath Influence[1]

⅏ RABBI SHIMON BAR YOCHAI RETURNS

It took an old man running with myrtle twigs to stop Rabbi Shimon bar Yochai from destroying the world.

The Talmud in *Shabbat* 33b relates how Rabbi Shimon bar Yochai and his son secreted themselves in a cave, hiding from the Romans. They spent twelve years secluded in Torah study and prayer, living off the fruit of a carob tree and fresh water from a spring.

When at last they heard that the Roman decree had been rescinded, Rabbi Shimon and his son left the cave. But years of seclusion had transformed the two scholars. When they saw people everywhere occupied with mundane activities, plowing fields and sowing grains, they were filled with outrage. "They forsake eternal life and engage in temporal life!" In their zeal, wherever they looked was immediately consumed by fire. Rabbi Shimon and his son were unable to reconcile themselves to the realities of everyday life, and a heavenly voice commanded them to return to their cave for an additional twelve months.

---

[1] Adapted from *Ein Ayah* vol. III on *Shabbat* 33b (2:278).

When they left the cave the second time, they came across an old man holding two twigs of myrtle branches. It was twilight, moments before the approach of the Sabbath, and the old man was running.

> "What are the myrtle twigs for?" inquired Rabbi Shimon.
> "They are in honor of the Sabbath," the old man replied.
> "But why two twigs?"
> "One is for *Zachor* ['Remember the Sabbath'] and the other is for *Shamor* ['Keep the Sabbath holy']."
> Rabbi Shimon turned to his son, "See how precious the mitzvot are to the people of Israel!" And their minds were put to ease.

What was it about the old man and his myrtle twigs that reconciled Rabbi Shimon bar Yochai and his son to the world and its mundane activities?

❧ SHAMOR AND ZACHOR

There are a number of differences in the text of the Ten Commandments as it appears in Exodus (in the reading of *Yitro)* and in Deuteronomy (in *Va'etchanan*). One difference is in the fourth command, the mitzvah of the Sabbath. In *Yitro* it reads *Zachor* – "Remember the Sabbath day" (Ex. 20:8) – while in *Va'etchanan* it reads *Shamor* – "Keep the Sabbath day holy" (Deut. 5:12). According to the Sages, these two versions are two sides of the same coin. Both *Shamor* and *Zachor* were communicated in a single Divine utterance. "God spoke once, but I heard twice" (Ps. 62:12).

Shamor and *Zachor* correspond to two basic aspects of the Sabbath. *Shamor*, keeping the Sabbath holy, refers to the quality of the Sabbath itself as a time of holiness. It corresponds to the intrinsic sanctity of the day, transcending all mundane activities, elevating us to a higher realm of holiness.

Zachor, to remember the Sabbath, on the other hand, refers to the Sabbath's influence on the other days of the week. While we fulfill the mitzvah of *Shamor* by abstaining from all forms of Halachically defined work on the Sabbath, the mitzvah of *Zachor* is performed during the week. As the Sages explained in *Mechilta Yitro*, if one comes across an especially choice portion of food, one should "Remember the Sabbath" and set it aside to be enjoyed on Shabbat.[2]

Zachor thus represents the power of the Sabbath to draw forth the energy of the days of worldly activity and elevate them with its special holiness. True, this is just a reminder of the Sabbath, and during the week we are primarily occupied with mundane pursuits. Yet the soul is naturally drawn to holiness, and the quest for a higher purpose in life is ingrained deep within us.

It was precisely this quality of *Zachor* that enabled Rabbi Shimon and his son to look upon everyday life in a positive light. The very fact that the Sabbath is able to influence the days of work reveals the soul's innate closeness to God.

⋈ HONORING THE SABBATH

Now many of the details in the story may be understood. Why the emphasis on the twilight hour? Why was the old man running? What is the significance of the myrtle twigs?

Twilight (*bein hashemashot*) is a bridge between one day and the next. Twilight between Friday and the Sabbath is the hour that connects the secular week with the holiness of Shabbat. The old man was running to honor the Sabbath at twilight on Friday eve; his action reflected the influence of the Sabbath on the rest of the week by way of its connection to Shabbat.

Why did the old man honor the Sabbath with fragrant myrtle twigs? Superficially, the weekdays appear mundane and lowly. In truth, they contain an inner reserve of holiness, but this inner holiness can only be perceived with an acute spiritual sensitivity. The myrtle twigs reflect this heightened sensitivity, since we appreciate their fragrance through our sense of smell.

---

2   See Ramban on Ex. 20:7, who explained *Zachor* to mean that "on each day we should always remember the Sabbath, so that it will not be forgotten or confused with other days. For by always remembering [the Sabbath], we remember the creation of the world at all times and constantly acknowledge that the world has a Creator."

The Sages wrote that of the five senses, the sense of smell is the most refined, giving pleasure to the soul (*Berachot* 43b). The two twigs correspond to the two aspects of the Sabbath, one for *Zachor*, connecting the Sabbath with the rest of the week, and one for *Shamor*, guarding the Sabbath's inherent sanctity.

And what is the significance of the old man running? The elderly do not usually run; what gave him this youthful energy and vitality? As the old man held the fragrant myrtle twigs in his hands, he felt the holy influence of the Sabbath on the other days of the week. This unusual combination of an old man running is a metaphor for the synthesis of the Sabbath, with its innate holiness and wisdom, and the weekdays, with their energy and productivity.

❧ COMBINING TEMPORAL WITH ETERNAL

We must still clarify: how did this sight enable Rabbi Shimon bar Yochai and his son to accept the mundane activities of everyday life?

The key lies in Rabbi Shimon's statement, after witnessing how the old man honored the Sabbath: "See how precious the mitzvot are to the people of Israel!"

Rabbi Shimon was no longer troubled by the neglect of eternal values due to preoccupation with day-to-day activities. The striking image of an old man running to honor the Sabbath brought home the realization that the mitzvot are truly the inner life-force of our lives. The scholar saw that even in its everyday life, the Jewish people are tightly bound to eternal values. These binds give strength to the weak and weary, so that even the elderly are able to serve God with exuberance and vitality.

His profound disappointment with society was eased when he realized that the transformation of old age to youthful vitality is only possible when worldly activity transcends its ordinary boundaries and enters the realm of holiness. Not only was Rabbi Shimon able to accept the people's occupation with mundane pursuits, he now recognized the added value to be gained precisely through this wonderful combination of the temporal and the eternal.

ROSH HASHANAH
ראש השנה

Revealing the Inner Force of the Soul

תִּקְעוּ בַחֹדֶשׁ שׁוֹפָר, בַּכֶּסֶה, לְיוֹם חַגֵּנוּ (תהילים פא:ד)

"Blow the shofar on the new moon, in the hidden time, on our festival day" (Ps. 81:4).

In the new start of the year, the force of renewal bestows holiness to living things, similar to the hour when they were first created. The inner force hidden in our soul is also revealed, advancing the soul in thought and deed.[1]

(Mo'adei HaRe'iyah, p. 60)

---

1   Rosh Hashanah is the only holiday occurring at the beginning of the month, when the moon is hidden. For this reason the verse refers to Rosh Hashanah as the festival that takes place at "the hidden time." The call of the shofar is a call of renewal, a call to reveal the soul's hidden inner forces.

Unity and Repentance[1]

S WE STAND before the start of a new year, it is incumbent upon us to examine our deeds and aspire to the path of *teshuvah* (repentance), a path that brings redemption and healing to the world.

The Jewish people have become divided into two camps, through the categorization of Jews as *Charedi* (religious) and *Chofshi* (secular). These are new terms, which were not used in the past. Of course, not everyone is identical, especially in spiritual matters; but there was never a specific term to describe each faction. In this respect, we can certainly say that previous generations were superior to ours.

By emphasizing this categorization, we obstruct the path toward improvement and growth in both camps. Those who feel that they belong to the religious camp look down upon the secular camp. If they think about *teshuvah* and improvement, they immediately cast their eyes in the direction of the secularists, devoid of Torah and mitzvot. They are confident that full repentance is required by the irreligious, not by them.

The secular Jews, on the other hand, are convinced that any notion of penitence is a religious concept, completely irrelevant to their lives.

It would be better if we would all concentrate on examining our own

---

1 Adapted from *Mo'adei HaRe'iyah*, p. 58, originally published in the journal *HaYesod*, 1933.

defects, and judge others generously. It could very well be that others have treasure-troves of merits, hidden from sight. We should recognize that there exists in each camp a latent force leading toward goodness. Each camp has much to improve upon, and could learn much from the positive traits of the other camp.

Let us be known to each other by one name – *Klal Yisrael*. And let our prayer be fulfilled: "וְיֵעָשׂוּ כֻלָּם אֲגֻדָּה אֶחָת לַעֲשׂוֹת רְצוֹנְךָ בְּלֵבָב שָׁלֵם" – "May they all become *one brotherhood*, to fulfill Your Will whole-heartedly" (from the High Holiday liturgy).

The Teshuvah of Rosh Hashanah[1]

T HE PRIMARY THEME of the month of Elul and the High Holiday season is *teshuvah* – repentance and return to God. Yet if we examine the Rosh Hashanah prayers, there is no mention of sin or penitence. There are no confessional prayers, no promises to improve. Instead, the Rosh Hashanah prayers deal with a completely different subject: universal acceptance of God's sovereignty. How does this aspiration fit in with the seasonal theme of *teshuvah*?

❧ FROM MY STRAITS

Before blowing the shofar on Rosh Hashanah, we recite the verse from Psalms:

מִן־הַמֵּצַר קָרָאתִי יָּ-הּ, עָנָנִי בַמֶּרְחָב יָ-הּ. (תהילים קיח:ה)

From my straits I called out to God; He answered me and set me in a wide expanse. (Ps. 118:5)

The verse begins with narrow *straits*, and concludes with wide *expanses*. What are these straits? These are our troubled, even suffocating, feelings of failure and disappointment with ourselves. However, with God's help we are

---

1   Adapted from *Mo'adei HaRe'iyah*, p. 60.

45

able to escape to "wide expanses." Our sense of confinement is eased and our emotional distress is alleviated.

This progression from the narrow to the wide is also a good physical description of the principle mitzvah-object of Rosh Hashanah – the shofar, which gradually expands from a narrow mouthpiece to a wide opening.

❧ FROM THE INDIVIDUAL TO THE COMMUNITY

Rav Kook, however, did not explain this progression from narrow to wide in a psychological vein. Rather, he likened it to the contrast between the *prat* and the *klal*, the individual and the collective. There are the narrow, private issues of the individual. And there are the broad, general concerns of the community and the nation.

Teshuvah takes place on many levels. We all try to correct our own personal faults and failings. The nation also does *teshuvah* as it restores itself to its native land, renewing its language, culture, and beliefs. And the entire world advances as it learns to recognize God's moral rule and sovereignty.

The shofar, with its gradually widening shape, is a metaphor for these ever-expanding circles of repentance and spiritual progress. The order, however, is significant. Our individual *teshuvah* must precede the universal *teshuvah* of the *klal*. During the month of Elul, we are occupied with rectifying our own personal faults and errors. But on Rosh Hashanah our outlook broadens. We yearn for the *teshuvah* of the Jewish people and the ultimate repair of the entire universe. We aspire "to perfect the world under the reign of the Almighty, when all humanity will call out Your Name" (from the *Aleinu* prayer in *Musaf* of Rosh Hashanah). From the narrow straits of personal limitations, we progress to the wide expanses of universal perfection.

Personal Judgment[1]

   NINE BLESSINGS

The longest prayer of the year is the *Musaf* prayer of Rosh Hashanah. The Talmud in *Berachot* 29a teaches that this prayer is connected to Hannah, the mother of the prophet Samuel:

> Why are there nine blessings in the Rosh Hashanah prayer? Because Hannah mentioned God's Name nine times in her prayers for a son. For it was taught: [The prayers of] Sarah, Rachel, and Hannah were answered on Rosh Hashanah.

Rosh Hashanah, at the start of the new year, is a time when all creatures are judged by God. The Sages used the imagery of a shepherd who inspects his sheep as they pass, one by one, under his staff. Such is God's judgment on Rosh Hashanah; the Divine inspection is not only on the level of nations and species, but also for each individual.

What is the significance of the number nine? If we analyze numbers, we find that ten indicates a unit that is also a group of smaller units. The number nine, on the other hand, emphasizes the individuality of each unit,

---

1   Adapted from *Ein Eyah* vol. I on *Berachot* 29a (4:44).

without being combined into a larger group. Nine is therefore an excellent choice for a number emphasizing the aspect of Rosh Hashanah as a time of personal judgment for each individual.

❧ HANNAH'S PRAYER

Is there a deeper connection between Hannah and our Rosh Hashanah prayer? Hannah was naturally barren. Medically, she was incapable of bearing a child. Yet she pleaded for a child by virtue of her personal merits and intense yearnings. She beseeched God for special assistance, beyond that which was decreed on a general, natural basis. Hannah's prayers truly exemplify the aspect of Divine providence for the individual, to the extent that Divine intervention was necessary in order to fulfill her request.

Especially on Rosh Hashanah, we need to impress upon ourselves how God judges each individual. When we are able to truly internalize this concept, we are motivated to correct our deeds and actions. And the moral elevation of each individual will bring about the overall repair of society and the entire world.

The Call of the Great Shofar[1]

Rav Kook delivered the following sermon in Jerusalem's Old City on Rosh Hashanah 1933. It was a time of mixed tidings. On the one hand, iominous news of Hitler's reign in Germany became more troubling with each passing day. On the other hand, the Jewish community in Eretz Yisrael was flourishing. Immigration from central Europe was increasing, bringing educated immigrants with needed skills and financial means. It seemed that the footsteps of redemption could be heard.

WE SAY IN our daily prayers, "תְּקַע בְּשׁוֹפָר גָּדוֹל לְחֵרוּתֵנוּ, וְשָׂא נֵס לְקַבֵּץ גָּלֻיּוֹתֵינוּ" – "Sound the great shofar for our freedom, and raise the banner to bring our exiles together." What is the significance of this "great shofar"?

✿ THREE SHOFARS

There are three types of shofars that may be blown on Rosh Hashanah. The optimal shofar is the horn of a ram. If a ram's horn is not available, then the horn of any kosher animal other than a cow may be used. And if a kosher shofar is not available, then one may blow on the horn of any animal,

[1] Adapted from *Mo'adei HaRe'iyah*, pp. 67–70.

even one which is not kosher. When using a horn from a non-kosher animal, however, no blessing is recited.

These three shofars of Rosh Hashanah correspond to three "Shofars of Redemption," three Divine calls summoning the Jewish people to be redeemed and to redeem their land.

The preferred Shofar of Redemption is the Divine call that awakens and inspires the people with holy motivations, through faith in God and the unique mission of the people of Israel. This elevated awakening corresponds to the ram's horn, a horn that recalls Abraham's supreme love of God and dedication in *Akeidat Yitzchak*, the Binding of Isaac. It was the call of this shofar, with its holy vision of heavenly Jerusalem united with earthly Jerusalem, that inspired Nachmanides, Rabbi Yehuda HaLevy, Rabbi Ovadia of Bartenura, the students of the Vilna Gaon, and the disciples of the Baal Shem Tov to ascend to *Eretz Yisrael*. It is for this "great shofar," an awakening of spiritual greatness and idealism, that we fervently pray.

There exists a second Shofar of Redemption, a less optimal form of awakening. This shofar calls out to the Jewish people to return to their homeland, to the land where our ancestors, our prophets and our kings, once lived. It beckons us to live as a free people, to raise our families in a Jewish country and a Jewish culture. This is a kosher shofar, albeit not a great shofar like the first type of awakening. We may still recite a *brachah* over this shofar.

There is, however, a third type of shofar. (At this point in the sermon, Rav Kook burst out in tears.) The least desirable shofar comes from the horn of an unclean animal. This shofar corresponds to the wake-up call that comes from the persecutions of anti-Semitic nations, warning the Jews to escape while they still can and flee to their own land. Enemies force the Jewish people to be redeemed, blasting the trumpets of war, bombarding them with deafening threats of harassment and torment, giving them no respite. The shofar of unclean beasts is thus transformed into a Shofar of Redemption.

Whoever failed to hear the calls of the first two shofars will be forced to listen to the call of this last shofar. Over this shofar, however, no blessing is recited. "One does not recite a blessing over a cup of affliction" (*Berachot* 51b).

·❧· THE GREAT SHOFAR

We pray that we will be redeemed by the "great shofar." We do not wish to be awakened by the calamitous call of the shofar of persecution, nor by the mediocre shofar of ordinary national aspirations. We yearn for the shofar that is suitable for a holy nation, the shofar of spiritual greatness and true freedom. We await the shofar blasts of complete redemption, the sacred call inspiring the Jewish people with the holy ideals of Jerusalem and Mount Moriah:

> On that day a great shofar will be blown, and the lost from the land of Assyria and the dispersed from the land of Egypt will come and bow down to God in the holy mountain in Jerusalem. (Isaiah 27:13)

The Dual Call of the Shofar[1]

THE CENTRAL MITZVAH of Rosh Hashanah is to hear the blasts of
the shofar. The ram's horn is blown twice during the holiday service:
first, immediately before the *Musaf* prayer, and a second time during
the *Musaf* prayer. Why do we need two sets of shofar blasts?

✍ TESHUVAH OF THE MIND AND HEART

The prophet Isaiah taught those who wish to return to God:

דִּרְשׁוּ ה' בְּהִמָּצְאוֹ, קְרָאֻהוּ בִּהְיוֹתוֹ קָרוֹב. (ישעיהו נ"ה:ו)

Seek out God where He is found. Call out to Him when He is near.
(Isaiah 55:6)

What is the difference between these two aspects of *teshuvah* – "seeking
out God" and "calling out to Him"?

First it is necessary to "seek out God." We need to restore the soul's
inner light, dimmed by character faults and misdeeds. Before losing our
way, we felt a joy in serving God. We recognized God's greatness and were
delighted with the opportunity to study His Torah and fulfill His mitzvot.
Sin, however, darkens the mind and numbs the heart, causing us to lose the

---

1   Adapted from *Midbar Shur*, pp. 56–58.

wonderful revelations from God's immanence. Therefore, the first stage of *teshuvah* is to "seek out God" – an *intellectual* striving to recover our former enlightenment and restore our joy in knowing God and His ways.

The second area that must be repaired is in the realm of the *emotions*, to restore the lost feeling of God's closeness and protection, the perception of Divine favor in material and spiritual matters. To recover this loss, we must "call out to God" and reach out to Him in prayer. We need to overcome our emotional estrangement and restore our sense of God's intimacy.

FOCUS THE MIND, OPEN THE HEART

The shofar is the tool that helps us accomplish both of these goals, seeking out God with the mind and calling to Him with the heart.

The first set of blasts is blown before praying the Rosh Hashanah *Musaf* prayer. They are called *tekiyot demeyushav*, "blasts while sitting," as they correspond to the *teshuvah* of the mind: a composed and thoughtful introspection on our insignificance and God's infinite greatness. *Demeyushav* comes from the Hebrew word for "sitting" – *yeshivah* – which also means an academy of Torah study. These blasts inspire us to contemplate God and His ways, to *"seek out God where He is found."*

The second set of shofar blasts takes place during the *Musaf* prayer. These blasts are called *tekiyot deme'umad*, "blasts while standing." They are an integral part of the prayer service. *Deme'umad* comes from the Hebrew word for "standing" – *amidah* – which is also the name of the central prayer, recited while standing. These shofar blasts are like prayer; they are an emotional service of God that fills us with awe and humility. They remind us to reconnect to God with our hearts, to feel His closeness and protection, to *"call out to Him when He is near."*

The Music of Teshuvah[1]

WHAT IS THE significance of the various blasts of the shofar? The shofar is a wake-up call, stirring us to mend our ways and do *teshuvah*. As Maimonides wrote in the *Mishneh Torah*, the shofar calls out to us: "*Sleepers, wake up from your slumber! Examine your ways and repent and remember your Creator*" (Laws of Repentance 3:4). Thus when looking for an explanation of the shofar blasts, we should examine ideas that are connected to this theme of spiritual awakening.

✂ THREE LEVELS

The initial blast of the shofar is a long, constant sound called a *tekiyah*. This simple call relates to the soul's inner source of holiness, its innate connection to God. The soul's inner essence is rooted in an elevated realm that is "infinitely good and infinitely long," musically represented by the long, clear *tekiyah* blast.

However, this inner holiness should not remain concealed within the soul. Spiritual awakening means that this holiness is expressed in character traits and actions. Therefore the long *tekiyah* blast is followed by a series of shorter blasts, called *shevarim*. The fragmented sounds of the *shevarim*

---

1 Adapted from *Olat Re'iyah* vol. II, pp. 326–327.

correspond to the process of the inner soul expressing itself in particular character traits. Unlike the broad strokes of abstract concepts, the soul's enlightened glimpses of Divine ideals, our traits are more defined and specific – kindness and generosity, integrity and resolve, and so on. Thus the *shevarim* consist of a series of broken blasts, shorter than the *tekiyah*.

Yet we are not content with only refining character traits. Our spiritual awakening should also elevate our actions and deeds. Therefore the *shevarim* are followed by even shorter blasts, the staccato beat sounds called *teruah*. Since actions are even more detailed than traits – specific behaviors that express the qualities of kindness, integrity, and so on – they are audially represented by the rapid trill of the *teruah*.

In summary: we focus on the soul's inner essence (the *tekiyah*) in order to influence and refine the character traits (the *shevarim*), which in turn guide and elevate the actions (the *teruah*).

✣ THE FINAL *TEKIYAH*

Each set of shofar blasts concludes with a final *tekiyah*. Like the first *tekiyah*, this *tekiyah* represents the soul's core holiness. But while the first *tekiyah* signifies this inner essence as a potential force, the final *tekiyah* indicates the actualization of its impact on our traits and deeds.

✣ PARTIAL *TESHUVAH*

This explanation describes the complete set of shofar blasts – *tekiyah-shevarim-teruah-tekiyah*. However, we also blow two partial sets of shofar blasts, with only *shevarim* or *teruah* in the middle. What do these series of blasts represent?

Ideally, both our traits and our actions should be guided by the soul's inner holiness. But there are also situations of incomplete spiritual awakening. Some individuals may behave properly, but fail to refine their character traits. This situation is represented by the set of *tekiyah-teruah-tekiyah*, since only the *teruah* blasts (i.e., the actions) are influenced by the inner holiness of the *tekiyah*.

In other cases, there may be internal or external obstacles that prevent the inner soul from expressing itself in action. Nonetheless, there may still be a refinement of character traits. This situation is represented by the set of *tekiyah-shevarim-tekiyah*, as only the *shevarim* (the traits) are influenced by the *tekiyah*.

Clearly, the optimal situation is when the inner holiness is able to penetrate all levels, encompassing *shevarim* as well as *teruah*, both character traits and deeds. This ideal state is expressed in the psalmist's praise of those who recognize the importance of the *teruah* and know how to realize their inner holiness in their "walk," i.e., their practical path in life:

אַשְׁרֵי הָעָם יֹדְעֵי תְרוּעָה; ה', בְּאוֹר־פָּנֶיךָ יְהַלֵּכוּן. (תהילים פט:טז)

Fortunate is the nation that knows the *teruah*-blast; O God, they will walk in the light of Your countenance. (Ps. 89:16)

Knowing the *Teruah*-Blast[1]

THE ORDER OF the shofar blasts on Rosh Hashanah may be understood as corresponding to major stages in the history of the universe. There are two basic types of shofar blasts:

Tekiyah – one long, constant blast.
Shevarim-teruah – several short blasts followed by numerous staccato blows.

The shofar blasts are organized in sets of *tekiyah, shevarim-teruah, tekiyah.* First we blow one long blast, then several broken and staccato blasts, and then a long concluding blast. What do the different blasts symbolize, and why this particular order?

✺ PAST, PRESENT, AND FUTURE

All of history may be divided up into three stages, corresponding to the three parts of the prayer: ה' מֶלֶךְ, ה' מָלָךְ, ה' יִמְלֹךְ לְעוֹלָם וָעֶד – "God reigns; God reigned; God will reign forever."

"God reigned." This refers to God's absolute sovereignty in the past, before the sin of Adam. This is the first *tekiyah*, the pure clarion call of a

---

1 Adapted from *Mo'adei HaRe'iyah,* pp. 62–63.

pristine world. The word *tekiyah* comes from the root *taku'a*, meaning "set" or "fixed in place."

Likewise, in the end of days, the era of the *tekiyah* will return. After all the tribulations over time, the simple, unwavering *tekiyah* will be heard once again, as the entire world will recognize God's rule. This is the future era of "God will reign forever."

❧ KNOWING THE *TERUAH*

In between the two constant *tekiyah* blasts, however, comes the complex intermediate stage. This is the current reality, a world that struggles to implement the ideal of "God reigns." This difficult stage is represented by the broken *shevarim* blows and the sobbing of the *teruah* blasts (*shever* means "broken" and *ra'uah* means "shaky"). It is a time of volatility and uncertainty, an era characterized by advances and setbacks, progress and failure.

This is the meaning of the verse, "Fortunate is the nation that knows the *teruah*" (Ps. 89:16). Fortunate are those who know how to cope with the challenges of this world, who know how to transcend the *teruah* blasts of uncertainty and hardship. Despite the doubts and confusion, they are able to "walk in the light of Your Presence" (ibid.), in the knowledge that the future era of "God will reign forever" lies ahead.

꩜

Awakening the Mind and Heart[1]

⋙ *YOM TERUAH*

The Torah describes Rosh Hashanah as a יוֹם תְּרוּעָה, "a day of *teruah*-blasts" (Num. 29:1). What are these *teruah*-blasts of the shofar? What is their connection to Rosh Hashanah and the High Holiday theme of repentance and return?

According to the Talmud in *Rosh Hashanah* 34a, the exact sound of the *teruah* is a matter of dispute. Some say it is *genuchei ganach*, a groaning or moaning sound. According to this opinion, the *teruah* should be heavy, broken sounds called *shevarim*, like the sobs of a soul burdened with remorse and regret.

Others, however, say that the *teruah* is *yelulei yalil*, trembling cries and wails. This opinion holds that the blasts should be short, staccato bursts, like the uncontrolled wailing of a person in extreme anguish and grief.

What is the significance of this dispute? What does it matter whether the shofar sounds like groans or howls?

---

1 Adapted from *Olat Re'iyah* vol. II, pp. 328–329.

❧ STIMULUS FOR CHANGE

When we examine individuals who have undergone great spiritual transformation, we find two basic patterns. For some people, change was initiated by a carefully considered process of logic and reason. Intellectually they realized that something was seriously amiss in their lives, and they sought to correct it. For others, on the other hand, the principle motive for change came from the heart. They were moved by a strong intuitive feeling that they had lost their true path, an overwhelming sense that their life had failed to fulfill their heart's aspirations.

We might ask: which stimulus is truly fundamental to the *teshuvah* process? Which path is more successful in sustaining spiritual growth – through the cognitive analysis of the mind or through the stirrings of the heart?

This question is precisely the doubt regarding the sound of the *teruah*. The shofar-blasts are a wake-up call for change and *teshuvah*. As Maimonides wrote in the *Mishneh Torah* (Laws of Repentance 3:4),

> It is as if the shofar is calling out to us: "Sleepers, wake up from your slumber! Examine your ways and repent and remember your Creator."

Perhaps the shofar blasts should recall the heavy sighs of the introspective individual who realizes that his life's direction is false. The shofar should sound like *genuchei ganach*, the groans of one whose objective assessments have lead him to the unavoidable conclusion that he has missed the mark in his life and goals. Or perhaps the shofar blasts are meant to mirror the emotional outburst of *yelulei yalil*, the cries of pain and anguish of one distraught by a torrent of emotions at losing his way.

❧ UTILIZING BOTH MIND AND HEART

There is, however, a third possibility. There is an ancient custom that the shofar blasts are meant to sound like both *genuchei ganach* and *yelulei yalil*. This opinion holds that we should blow *shevarim-teruah*, combining groans and uncontrollable weeping.

This custom reflects the most complete form of *teshuvah*, one that incorporates both the intellect and the emotions. One begins with *genuchei ganach*, a cognitive realization that all is not well and change is necessary. This intellectual awareness then fosters a sense of remorse and grief so vivid that it awakens the most powerful emotions – *yelulei yalil*. Maimonides similarly described the *teshuvah* process as progressing from cognitive decision to emotional remorse, "The sinner relinquishes the sin, removing it from his thoughts and resolving never to repeat it. . . . And then he should feel remorse for his past misdeeds" (Laws of Repentance 2:2).

This is the most effective form of *teshuvah*, as it utilizes the strengths of both faculties, the emotions and the intellect. The advantage of emotions over cold logic is their ability to make a deep impression on the soul. On the other hand, change based on emotions alone, without a reasoned foundation, may be unsustainable in the long run.

The psalmist exclaimed, "Fortunate is the nation that knows the *teruah*-blast!" (Ps. 89:16). What is so wonderful about knowing how the shofar sounds? Rather, the verse means this: when we understand the true power of the *teruah* – when we know how to utilize both aspects, the *genuchei*-sighs of the mind as well as the *yelulei*-cries of the heart – then we can base our *teshuvah* on the solid foundation of reason and emotions together. With such *teruah*-blasts, "they will walk in the light of Your countenance" (ibid.) – we are assured of following a path of life enlightened by God's light.

꙰

Blasts That Penetrate the Heart[1]

"FORTUNATE IS THE nation that knows the *teruah*-blast" (Psalms 89:16). What is so special about recognizing the sound of the shofar? Rav Kook explained in *Olat Re'iyah* (vol. II, p. 329) that in the shofar-blasts, one may hear the inner call of *teshuvah*:

This idea is illustrated in the following story.

꙰ THE WAKE-UP CALL

In one of the neighborhoods of Jerusalem, a group of workers was under pressure to complete a particular building, and they continued working during the Rosh Hashanah holiday.

When the neighbors realized what was happening, they immediately notified Rav Kook. Shortly thereafter, a messenger of the Rav arrived at the construction site – with a shofar in his hand. He approached the workers, who were surprised to see him, and offered New Year's greetings. He then announced that Rav Kook had sent him to blow the shofar for them, in accordance with the obligation to hear the shofar on Rosh Hashanah. He respectfully asked them to take a break from their work and listen. The messenger then proceeded to recite the blessing and began to blow.

---

1 Adapted from *Mo'adei HaRe'iyah*, pp. 65–66.

The words from the Rav and the sounds of the shofar achieved their goal. Each blast shook the delicate chords of the soul and awakened the Jewish spark in the hearts of the young workers. They set down their work tools and gathered around the man blowing the shofar. Some were so moved that they began to cry. The ancient blasts of the shofar, reverberating in the unfinished building, transported them back to their father's house. They saw images of grandfather, the shtetl and the synagogue, a world of Jews standing in prayer.

Questions began to pour out, one after another. *What has happened to us? Where are we? What have we come to?* The young men stood around the emissary, confused and absorbed in thought.

When the shofar-blowing was over, there was no need for words. The workers unanimously decided to stop working. Some asked the messenger if they could accompany him. They quickly changed their clothes and joined in the holiday prayers at Rav Kook's yeshivah.

In an open letter from that time, Rav Kook wrote:

> A friendly word is effective; an expression of comradeship and respect will bring others close. Let us not forsake the good and straight path that is illuminated with love and goodwill, peace and friendship. We must break down the wall that divides brothers and speak heart to heart, soul to soul; then our words will certainly be heard. And these sons of ours will suddenly raise themselves up, and they will crown their powerful aspiration to build the land and the nation with the eternal ideals of sublime holiness.

YOM KIPPUR
יום הכיפורים

The Threefold Nature of Yom Kippur

Yom Kippur is the inner content of the entire year. For this reason it is called אַחַת בַּשָּׁנָה – "Once in the year" (Lev. 16:34). It is the one and singular trait that illuminates the entire year.

[Yom Kippur] contains three aspects:

The day's own intrinsic value as a sublime and holy day with its own special light;

Its value in elevating the year that passed;

Its value in elevating the year to come.[1]

(*Olat Re'iyah* vol. 1, pp. 139–140)

1   Once a year, 368 measures of *ketoret* (incense) were produced for the Temple service – one measure for each day of the year, plus three extra measures for Yom Kippur (*Keritut* 6a). These three extra measures correspond to the three special spiritual qualities of the day.

The Holy King[1]

THE DAYS FROM Rosh Hashanah until Yom Kippur are called *Aseret Y'mei Teshuvah*, the Ten Days of Repentance. During this period, our relationship with God changes, as reflected in two changes in the *Amidah* prayer:

* Instead of referring to God as הָאֵ־ל הַקָּדוֹשׁ ("the Holy God"), we call Him הַמֶּלֶךְ הַקָּדוֹשׁ ("the Holy King").

* Instead of מֶלֶךְ אוֹהֵב צְדָקָה וּמִשְׁפָּט ("the King Who loves kindness and justice"), we pray to הַמֶּלֶךְ הַמִּשְׁפָּט ("the King of justice").

What is the significance of these changes?

҂ DIVINE RULE DURING THE TEN DAYS OF *TESHUVAH*

God governs the world in a different fashion during the Ten Days of *Teshuvah*. Throughout the year, His rule is revealed through the attribute of *Elokut* (Godliness); but during this special time, He rules with the attribute of *Malchut* (Kingship). What does this mean?

A king judges his subjects according to their current state, deciding

---

1 Adapted from *Olat Re'iyah* vol. I, pp. 272–273.

who deserves punishment and who deserves reward. In the Divine rule of *Malchut*, evil is not tolerated.

In the elevated Divine view of *Elokut*, on the other hand, everything has an ultimate purpose. Even the wicked, the Sages taught, contribute to God's praise (*Shemot Rabbah* 7). It may be beyond our limited understanding, but evil also serves a purpose in the world. Ultimately, the wicked, through their free choice, bring grief only to themselves.

A holy individual is one who is able to elevate all of his actions, even those that are mundane and lowly. "All of your actions should be for the sake of Heaven" (*Avot* 2:15). Holiness means sanctifying all aspects of life. So, too, the Divine rule of *Elokut* encompasses all aspects of the world, even base and evil ones, with the knowledge that they will be ultimately rectified and elevated.

During the rest of the year, God suffers evil so that the wicked will have the opportunity to repair the harm they have done. We refer to God during the year as the "Holy God," since even base and wicked actions will, in the final analysis, lead to holy goals. This form of Divine rule emphasizes God's kindness and forbearance, and our prayers speak of God loving both justice and mercy.

During the Ten Days of *Teshuvah*, however, God is revealed as the "Holy King." The time has arrived for the wicked to mend their ways. If they fail to repent, they will be dealt with the attribute of *mishpat*, exacting judgment. During these ten days we experience God's providence as a King Who rejects all evil, so at this time, we refer to Him as "the King of judgment."

Eating Before Yom Kippur[1]

🙐 THE NINTH OF TISHREI

While there are several rabbinically ordained fasts throughout the year, only one day of fasting is mentioned in the Torah:

> It is a sabbath of sabbaths to you, when you must fast. You must observe this sabbath on the ninth of the month in the evening, from evening until [the next] evening. (Lev. 23:32)

This refers to the fast of Yom Kippur. The verse, however, appears to contain a rather blatant "mistake": Yom Kippur falls out on the tenth of Tishrei, not the ninth!

The Talmud in *Berachot* 8b explains that the day before Yom Kippur is also part of the atonement process, even though there is no fasting: "This teaches that one who eats and drinks on the ninth is credited as if he fasted on both the ninth and tenth."

Still, we need to understand: Why is there a mitzvah to eat on the day before Yom Kippur? In what way does this eating count as a day of fasting?

---

1 Adapted from *Ein Ayah* vol. I on *Berachot* 8b (1:103).

✺ TWO FORMS OF *TESHUVAH*

The theme of Yom Kippur is, of course, *teshuvah* – repentance, the soul's return to its innate purity. There are two major aspects to *teshuvah*. The first is the need to restore the soul's spiritual sensitivity, dulled by over-indulgence in physical pleasures. This refinement is achieved by temporarily rejecting physical enjoyment and replacing life's hectic pace with the quietude of prayer and introspection. The Torah gave us one day a year, the fast of Yom Kippur, to concentrate exclusively on refining our spirits and redirecting our lives.

However, the goal of Judaism is not asceticism. As Maimonides wrote in *Mishneh Torah,* Laws of Character Traits 3:1–4:

> One might say that since jealousy, lust, and arrogance are bad traits, driving a person out of the world, I will go to the opposite extreme. I will not eat meat, nor drink wine, nor marry, nor live in a nice house, nor wear fine clothing . . . like the gentile priests. This is wrong, and it is forbidden to act in this fashion. One who follows this path is called a sinner. . . . Therefore the Sages instructed that we should only restrict ourselves from that which the Torah forbids. . . . This includes those who constantly fast – they are not in the proper path. The Sages prohibited afflicting oneself with fasting.

The second aspect of *teshuvah* is more practical and functional. We need to become accustomed to acting properly and avoid the pitfalls of materialistic pursuits that distort the Torah's teachings. This level of *teshuvah* is not attained by fasts and meditation, but by preserving our spiritual and moral integrity *while* we are engaged in worldly matters.

The true goal of Yom Kippur is achieved when we are able to remain faithful to our spiritual essence while remaining active participants in the material world. When do we accomplish this aspect of *teshuvah*? When we eat on the ninth of Tishrei. Then we demonstrate that, despite our occupation with physical activities, we can remain faithful to the Torah's values and ideals. Thus, our eating on the day before Yom Kippur is integrally connected to our fasting on Yom Kippur itself. Together, these two days correspond to the two corrective aspects of the *teshuvah* process.

By preceding the fast with a mitzvah to eat and drink, the Torah teaches that the reflection and spiritual refinement of Yom Kippur are not to be isolated to that one day, but connected to the entire year's involvement in the physical world. The inner, meditative *teshuvah* of the tenth of Tishrei is thus complemented by the practical *teshuvah* of the ninth.

Complete Teshuvah[1]

THE FOCUS OF the days between Rosh Hashanah and Yom Kippur is *teshuvah*. We recite the *Avinu Malkeinu* prayer during this period, requesting:

אָבִינוּ מַלְכֵּנוּ! הַחֲזִירֵנוּ בִּתְשׁוּבָה שְׁלֵמָה לְפָנֶיךָ.

Our Father our King! Return us in complete *teshuvah* before You.

When is *teshuvah* full and complete?

✦ HEALING THE SOURCE

We may understand this phrase better in light of the request that immediately follows: "Our Father our King! Send complete healing to the sick of Your people."

What is "complete healing"? Often we are only able to alleviate the patient's external symptoms. The true source of the illness, however, remains unknown or is untreatable. Such a treatment is only a partial healing. When we plead for complete healing, we are praying that we may succeed in discovering the source of the illness and completely cure the patient. Such a comprehensive treatment will result in full restoration of the patient's health.

---

1   Adapted from *Mo'adei HaRe'iyah*, p. 66.

The same concept holds true for *teshuvah*. If we address a particular fault, we are really dealing with a symptom of a much larger problem. Correcting a specific sin is only partial *teshuvah*. When we ask for God's help in attaining complete *teshuvah*, we seek a comprehensive *teshuvah* that repairs the root source of our various sins and character flaws. Such a complete *teshuvah* will restore our spiritual wholeness.

❧ ELEVATED PERCEPTION

How does one attain complete *teshuvah*? In his book *Orot HaTeshuvah*, Rav Kook explained that this *teshuvah* is based on an elevated outlook on life and the world:

> The higher level of *teshuvah* is based on holy enlightenment and a penetrating perception of the beauty of Divine providence. This [elevated *teshuvah*] is the source and foundation for the lower *teshuvah* that corrects deeds and refines traits. The basis for elevated *teshuvah* is none other than the foundation of Torah, in all of its roots and branches. (15:6)
>
> *Teshuvah* that is truly complete requires a lofty perception, an ascent to the rarified world that is replete with truth and holiness. This is only possible by delving into the depths of Torah and Divine wisdom, to the mystical secrets of the universe .... Only the higher [i.e., mystical] Torah can break down the iron barriers that divide the individual and society as a whole from their heavenly Father.[2] (10:1)

---

2   However, in *Orot HaTeshuvah* 4:9, Rav Kook cautioned about the dangers of studying the Torah's mystical teachings without proper preparation.

꩜

"You Know the Mysteries of the Universe"[1]

BEFORE RECITING THE Yom Kippur *viduy* (confessional prayer), we offer a special prayer:

אַתָּה יוֹדֵעַ רָזֵי עוֹלָם וְתַעֲלוּמוֹת סִתְרֵי כָּל חָי. אַתָּה חוֹפֵשׂ כָּל חַדְרֵי בָטֶן וּבוֹחֵן כְּלָיוֹת וָלֵב. אֵין דָּבָר נֶעְלָם מִמֶּךָ, וְאֵין נִסְתָּר מִנֶּגֶד עֵינֶיךָ. וּבְכֵן יְהִי רָצוֹן מִלְּפָנֶיךָ ה' אֱלֹהֵינוּ וֵאלֹהֵי אֲבוֹתֵינוּ, שֶׁתִּסְלַח לָנוּ עַל כָּל חַטֹּאתֵינוּ, וְתִמְחָל לָנוּ עַל כָּל עֲווֹנוֹתֵינוּ, וּתְכַפֶּר לָנוּ עַל כָּל פְּשָׁעֵינוּ.

You know the mysteries of the universe and the hidden secrets of every living soul. You search the innermost chambers of the conscience and the heart. Nothing escapes You; nothing is hidden from Your sight. Therefore, may it be Your Will to forgive all our sins.

Why do we introduce the Yom Kippur *viduy* by acknowledging God's infinite knowledge? What does God's knowledge of the hidden mysteries of the universe have to do with our efforts to repent and atone for our deeds?

ఒ THREE COMPONENTS OF *TESHUVAH*

There are three components to the *teshuvah* process, corresponding to the past, the present, and the future. *Teshuvah* should include (1) regret for

---

1   Adapted from *Olat Re'iyah* vol. II, p. 353.

74

improper conduct in the past, (2) a decision to cease this conduct in the present, and (3) resolve not to repeat it in the future.

And yet, as we shall shortly demonstrate, complete performance of all three aspects of *teshuvah* requires profound knowledge. In fact, *teshuvah sheleimah*, complete repentance, requires a level of knowledge far beyond our limited capabilities.

✖ REGRETTING THE PAST

For example, only if we are fully aware of the seriousness of our actions will we truly feel remorse over our past failings. The Kabbalists taught that our actions can influence the highest spiritual realms. The more we are aware of the damage caused by our wrongdoings, the greater will be our feelings of regret. For this reason the request for forgiveness in the daily *Amidah* prayer only appears *after* the request for knowledge. Certainly, the one most aware of the significance and impact of our actions is the One Who created the universe and all of the spiritual worlds.

✖ UPROOTING THE BEHAVIOR

The same is true regarding the second component of *teshuvah*. In order to completely free ourselves from a particular negative behavior or trait, it is not enough to desist from its outward manifestations. We need to remove all desire for this conduct; we need to dislodge its roots from the inner recesses of the soul. But how well do we know what resides in the depths of our heart? We may think that we have purified ourselves from a particular vice, and yet the disease is still entrenched within, and we will be unable to withstand a future re-awakening of this desire. The only one to truly know the inner chambers of our soul is the One Who created it.

✖ RESOLVE FOR THE FUTURE

The third component, our resolve to refrain from repeating this behavior in the future, means that we commit ourselves not to repeat our error, no matter what the situation, even under the most trying circumstances. Again, a full acceptance for the future implies knowledge of all future events and their impact upon us – a knowledge that is clearly denied to us. Only God knows the future.

So how can we aspire toward true *teshuvah*, when the essential components of the *teshuvah* process require knowledge that is beyond our limited abilities?

❧ COMPLETE *TESHUVAH*

God promises us that the mitzvah of *teshuvah* is within our grasp – "it is not too difficult or distant from you .... Rather, this matter is very close to you, in your mouth and in your heart, so that you can fulfill it" (Deut. 30:11–14). God graciously accepts the little we are able to accomplish as if it were much. We ask that the degree of regret, change, and resolve that we are capable of, even though it is limited by our capabilities, be combined with God's infinite knowledge. For if we were able to fully recognize matters in their true measure, we would feel them with all of their intensity in our efforts to better ourselves.

This then is the meaning of the Yom Kippur prayer:

"*You know the mysteries of the universe*" – only You know the full impact of our mistakes and how much remorse we should really feel – "*and the hidden secrets of every living soul*" – for we fail to properly regret our actions.

"*You search the innermost chambers of the conscience and the heart*" – You see that traces of our failings still lurk deep within us. Only You know to what degree we need to cleanse ourselves of character flaws that we have not fully succeeded in conquering.

"*Nothing escapes You; nothing is hidden from Your sight*" – You know all future events, including situations that will tempt us and perhaps cause us to stumble again.

Nonetheless, since we can only perform the various components of *teshuvah* according to our limited capabilities, we beseech God, "*May it be Your Will to forgive all of our sins.*" Then we can attain the level of "*complete repentance before You*" – a *teshuvah* that is complete when our sincere efforts are complemented by God's infinite knowledge.

Fulfilling Our Mission[1]

W E CONCLUDE THE *al cheit* confessional prayers of Yom Kippur with the following declaration:

אֱלֹהַי, עַד שֶׁלֹּא נוֹצַרְתִּי אֵינִי כְדַאי. וְעַכְשָׁיו שֶׁנּוֹצַרְתִּי כְּאִלּוּ לֹא נוֹצַרְתִּי.

My God, before I was formed, I was of no worth. And now that I have been formed, it is as if I was not formed.

The Talmud (*Berachot* 17a) records that fourth-century scholar Rava composed this prayer, but its meaning is unclear. Before I was formed, of course I was of no worth – I did not exist yet! And after I was formed – why does it say that "it is as if I was not formed"? Do I exist or not?

৺ MY LIFE'S GOAL

This short prayer gives us an important insight into the meaning of our existence.

"*Before I was formed, I was of no worth.*" Clearly, before I was born I was not needed in this world. "I was of no worth" – nothing required my existence, there was no mission for me to fulfill. Since I was not yet needed in the world, I was not born in an earlier generation.

[1] Adapted from *Olat Re'iyah* vol. II, p. 356.

"*And now that I have been formed*" – since my soul has entered the world at this point in time, it must be that now there is some mission for me to accomplish. I am needed to repair and complete some aspect of the world.

And yet, "*it is as if I was not formed.*" Were I to dedicate my life to fulfilling the purpose for which I was brought into the world, this would confirm and justify my existence. But since my actions are not in accordance with my true goal, I am not accomplishing my life's mission. And if I fail to fulfill my purpose in life, my very existence is called into question.

If I do not accomplish the mission for which I was placed in this world, then the situation has reverted back to its state before my birth, when, since I was not needed in the world, I was not yet formed. Thus, even now that I have been formed, it is regrettably "as if I was not formed."

THE MESSAGE FOR YOM KIPPUR

It is highly significant that this prayer was added to the Yom Kippur confession. After we have recognized and admitted our many faults and mistakes, we could conclude that we cause more harm than good, and would be better off retiring to the privacy of our homes. Rava's prayer teaches that we have a mission to accomplish, and it is critical that we discover this mission and work toward fulfilling it. Otherwise, tragically, "*it is as if I was not formed.*"

Healing the Universe[1]

T
HE SAGES MADE a startling claim about the power of *teshuvah*:

> Great is repentance, for it brings healing to the world. ... When an individual repents, he is forgiven, and the entire world with him. (*Yoma* 86b)

We understand that one who repents should be forgiven – but why should the entire world also be forgiven? In what way does *teshuvah* bring healing to the world?

❧ RESPONSIBILITY FOR THE WORLD

There are deep, powerful ties that connect each individual soul to the rest of the universe. Not only are we influenced by the world, we also influence it. In *Orot HaKodesh* (vol. II p. 351), Rav Kook described this connection as a "powerful underlying influence." This is not merely mankind's industrial and technological impact on the world, as we utilize fire, water, electricity, and other forces of nature to do our bidding.

> That is only a partial and superficial aspect of our impact on the world. The Kabbalists taught that the world's essence, in all of its wholeness and

---

1 Adapted from *Olat Re'iyah* vol. II, p. 364.

scope, is bound to us with ties of subordination, accepting our influence. This understanding indicates that there is a fundamental integration between the *nishmatiut* [soul-quality] that operates in the world and our own *nishmatiut*.

This inner connection and influence on the rest of the universe implies a heavy moral responsibility:

> How wonderful is the moral perspective that arises from this great responsibility – a responsibility for all of existence, for all worlds. We have the power to bring favor and light, life, joy, and honor in these worlds. This occurs when we follow the straight path, when we strengthen and gird ourselves with a pure fortitude and conquer paths of life that are good and admired, when we advance and go from strength to strength.
>
> Yet it is also in our power to bring pain to every good portion, when we debase our souls and corrupt our ways, when we darken our spiritual light and suspend our moral purity.   (*Orot HaKodesh* vol. III, p. 63)

Given our great responsibility for our actions, the Talmudic statement becomes clearer. Those who correct their ways repair not only the flaws in their own souls but also those aspects of the universe that they damaged. Their *teshuvah* truly "brings healing to the world."

✿   THE *NE'ILAH* PRAYER

This dual responsibility – for the purity of our souls as well as the spiritual state of the entire universe – is hinted at in the final prayer of Yom Kippur. The *Ne'ilah* prayer, recited as Yom Kippur's gates of forgiveness are closed, concludes with a special passage, אַתָּה נוֹתֵן יָד לַפּוֹשְׁעִים ("You extend Your hand to transgressors"). In this prayer we confess that

אֵין קֵץ לְאִשֵּׁי חוֹבוֹתֵינוּ וְאֵין מִסְפָּר לְנִיחוֹחֵי אַשְׁמָתֵנוּ.

There is no end to the fire-offerings required of us, and countless are our guilt-offerings.

What is the difference between these two phrases – "the fire-offerings required of us" (*ishei chovoteinu*) and "our guilt-offerings" (*nichochei ashmateinu*)?

✒ RESTORING THE SOUL'S PURITY

Our moral defects and lapses have a detrimental effect on the soul, sullying it with the imprints of failure and sin. We seek to cleanse these stains and restore the soul to its previous state of purity.

To repair the damage we have caused to our own soul, we offer an *olah* offering before God. It is for this reason that the Torah commands us to bring an offering even if we have sinned unintentionally.[2]

This *Ne'ilah* prayer refers to these offerings as *nichochei ashmateinu*, "guilt-offerings." This term indicates that our actions have tarnished the soul, as it says, "And the soul that was guilty (*ashmah*)" (Num. 5:6). These offerings are *nichochim* since they produce a "pleasing fragrance" as they cleanse the soul and enable it to once again draw close to God.

✒ REPAIRING THE WORLD

There is, however, a second aspect to our spiritual failures. In addition to defiling the soul, our sins also debase and pollute the universe. Even private failings have a negative impact on the moral and spiritual state of the universe. For this reason the Sages categorized the wicked as those "who destroy the world" (*Avot* 5:1).

The universe demands that we repair that which we have damaged. This repair is accomplished through *teshuvah* and offering a *chatat* offering. The *Ne'ilah* prayer refers to these offerings as *ishei chovoteinu*, "our *required* fire-offerings," since they reflect our duty and obligation to correct that which we have damaged in the universe.

---

2   So explained the Ramban (Rabbi Moses ben Nachman, 1194–1270), in his commentary to Lev. 4:2: "The reason that one who sinned unintentionally brings an offering (*korban*) is because all transgressions bring disgrace to the soul, tainting it . . . . Therefore a soul that erred brings an offering, so that it may merit to become close (*le-korvah*) to its Creator."

The Ox and the Goat[1]

THERE ARE MANY unique aspects to the Temple service on Yom Kippur. One special feature of Yom Kippur concerns the *chatat* sin-offerings. On all other holidays, a single sin-offering was brought, that of a goat. On Yom Kippur, however, there were two sin-offerings: an ox and a goat. What is the significance of these two animals, the ox and the goat?

FORGIVENESS FOR ALL ACTIONS

The ox is a symbol of great strength. Oxen were traditionally used for construction and cultivating land. The ox's strength was harnessed to till the earth, to transport goods, and for other constructive purposes.

The goat is also a symbol of power – but of a corrosive, destructive nature. The Hebrew word for goat (*sa'ir*) means to storm and rage. The foraging goat devours the very roots of the plants. Overgrazing by goats leads to land-erosion and destruction of pasture.

Both of these forms of power – constructive and destructive – may be used for positive goals, and both may be utilized for evil purposes. Each has its proper place and time. We use constructive forces to build and advance,

---

1   Adapted from *Olat Re'iyah* vol. I, p. 167.

and we need destructive forces when dismantling existing structures in order to rebuild and improve. Both types of forces, however, may be abused, causing much sorrow and grief.

The most common need for atonement is when we accidentally hurt or damage. For this reason, the standard *chatat* offering is the goat, a symbol of blight and destruction.

On Yom Kippur, however, we seek forgiveness for the misuse of *all* forms of power. Therefore, we offer a second *chatat* from an ox, the classic beast of labor. With this offering, we express our regret if, inadvertently, our constructive deeds may have been inappropriate or detrimental.

SUCCOTH סוכות

Waves of Joy

The *sukkah*-booth reflects a highly elevated joy, so lofty that it cannot be permanent, only temporary. Nonetheless it [appears to] be stationary due to a continual flow of light-waves of joy. One wave surges; then immediately, without interruption, it breaks and the next wave rushes forth, a new wave even brighter and more joyful. Thus, it appears to be one *sukkah*; but in fact, each second and each moment, there is truly a new *sukkah*.

Joy comes from renewal, and here the renewal is constant. Therefore this holiday is called "the Season of our Joy."[1]

(Arpilei Tohar, p. 52; Olat Re'iyah vol. II, p. 368; Mo'adei HaRe'iyah, p. 95)

---

1   In the liturgy, the holiday of Succoth is identified as זְמַן שִׂמְחָתֵנוּ, "the Season of our Joy." Joy is a major theme of the holiday, as it says, "You will rejoice in your holiday ... and you will be only happy" (Deut. 16:14–15).

Completing the Days of Awe[1]

W E REJOICE ON all of the holidays, but Succoth contains an exceptional measure of joy. In fact, this is the most prominent aspect of the holiday. Succoth is identified in the prayers as זְמַן שִׂמְחָתֵנוּ, "the Season of our Joy."

Why does this holiday of rejoicing immediately follow the High Holidays, Rosh Hashanah and Yom Kippur – a solemn period of introspection and penitence?

✤ RESTORING JOY

The process of purifying deeds and refining character traits naturally entails a certain dampening of the spirit. As we struggle to overcome negative personality traits, it is natural to lose some of life's innate spontaneity and joy. The corrective process of *teshuvah* can have the undesirable side effect of impairing the soul's positive and creative forces.

This phenomenon is analogous to a patient who underwent arduous chemotherapy treatment in order to eliminate a cancerous growth. The

---

1   Adapted from *Olat Re'iyah* vol. II, p. 368.

therapy in fact eradicated the deadly growth, but it also weakened healthy powers of the body.

Therefore, the holiday of Succoth — a time of elevated spirits and holy rejoicing – immediately follows the introspective Days of Awe. The Succoth festival restores the soul's wholesome sense of joy in life, and, in fact, completes the process of repentance and atonement.

All of Israel in One Sukkah[1]

THE TALMUD IN *Sukkah* 27b makes a remarkable claim regarding the holiday of Succoth:

"For seven days . . . all who belong to the people of Israel will live in *sukkot* [thatched huts]" (Lev. 23:42). This teaches that it is fitting for all of Israel to sit in one *sukkah*.

Obviously, no *sukkah* is large enough to hold the entire Jewish people. What is the meaning of this utopian vision – all of Israel sitting together in a single *sukkah*?

THE UNITY OF SUCCOTH

As long as we are plagued by pettiness and other character flaws, we cannot attain true collective unity. But after experiencing the unique holiness of Yom Kippur, this unfortunate state is repaired. After our lives have been illuminated by the light of *teshuvah* and the entire Jewish nation has been purified from the negative influences of sin and moral weakness, the soul's inner purity becomes our predominant quality. With this regained

---

1   Adapted from *Mo'adei HaRe'iyah*, p. 96.

integrity, we merit an ever-increasing harmony among the diverse sectors of the nation.

During the holiday of Succoth we absorb the light of Torah and a love for truth. Conflicting views become integrated and unified. Through the spiritual ascent of the Days of Awe, we attain a comprehensive unity, a unity that extends its holy light over all parts of the Jewish people. During this special time, it is as if the entire nation is sitting together, sharing the holy experience of the same *sukkah*.

According to the Hasidic master Rabbi Nathan,[2] this sense of unity is the very essence of the mitzvah of *sukkah*. He wrote in *Likutei Halachot* that one should fulfill the mitzvah of *sukkah* with the following *kavanah*:

> One should concentrate on being part of the entire people of Israel, with intense love and peace, until it may be considered as if all of Israel dwells together in one *sukkah*.

---

2 (1780–1844), chief disciple and scribe of Rabbi Nachman of Breslov.

Our Protective Fortress[1]

THE *SUKKAH* BOOTH that we live in during the Succoth holiday is by definition a temporary dwelling. The Sages ruled that a very tall structure, over ten meters high, is invalid as a *sukkah* because it is a permanent structure. An exposed hut consisting of only two walls and a handbreadth for the third, on the other hand, is perfectly acceptable.

And yet, this rickety booth is our protective fortress. As King David said, "You protect them in a *sukkah* from the strife of tongues" (Ps. 31:21). Why should such a flimsy structure be a paradigm of protection and safety?

❧ THE *SUKKOT* OF THE GREAT ASSEMBLY

To better understand the metaphor of the *sukkah*, we should examine a remarkable Talmudic passage. In Nehemiah 8:17 it states that, from the time of Joshua, the Jewish people had not dwelt in *sukkot* until the mitzvah was reinstated after their return from the Babylonian exile. How is it possible that this mitzvah was neglected for so many centuries?

The Talmud in *Arachin* 32b explains that the Jewish people always performed the mitzvah of dwelling in a *sukkah*. However, the *sukkot* erected by the Great Assembly in the time of Nehemiah were special *sukkot*,

---

1   Adapted from *Ma'amarei HaRe'iyah* vol. I, pp. 149–150.

possessing a protective quality that had not existed since the days of Joshua bin Nun. According to the Talmud, these were not even physical *sukkot*, but rather a unique spiritual act of Ezra and the Great Assembly: "They prayed and abolished the passion for idolatry, and this merit protected them like a *sukkah*."[2]

✑ THE ULTIMATE FORTRESS

Clearly, the protective aspect of the *sukkah* is of a spiritual nature. The eternal truth is that the *sukkah* – purposely defined as a structure so flimsy that it cannot even be called a proper dwelling – is a fortress that protects us from all adversaries and foes. What is it that transforms the exposed *sukkah* into a shelter and stronghold? Certainly not any of its physical properties. Rather, its source of inner strength is none other than God's word. *The sukkah protects us by virtue of the Torah law that declares this structure to be our shelter during the holiday of Succoth.*

This is an important message for all times, and especially in our generation. We need great courage to return to the land of our fathers and rebuild our national home. Where can we find the moral and spiritual resolve to withstand the challenges of those who oppose our return and deny our right to a homeland in *Eretz Yisrael*? Like the *sukkah* dwelling, our national home is based on the spiritual strength of God's eternal word. The most advanced weapons may be able to penetrate the thickest walls, but they cannot prevail over the stronghold of God's word.

This is our fortress, our ultimate shelter of security: God's eternal promise that the Jewish people will return to their land and the House of Israel will be built once again.

The protective *sukkah* of the Great Assembly was the merit provided by their spiritual efforts to abolish the desire for idolatry. Our right to the land of Israel is similarly based, not on our military prowess, but on the moral

---

2   Rav Kook would often quote an alternative solution to this question, the explanation of the Malbim (Rabbi Meir Leibush Weiser, 1809–1879), that the verse refers to *sukkot* for public use that for legal reasons were not erected during the First Temple Period.

strength of our eternal covenant with God and the merit of the Torah's mitzvot.

❧ BEAUTIFYING THE LAW

However, we should not be satisfied with keeping only the minimum requirements of Torah law. Jerusalem was destroyed, the Sages taught, because the judges ruled according to the strict letter of the law. They failed to take into account the spirit of the law and seek a ruling that is both just and compassionate – *lifnim mishurat hadin* (*Baba Metzi'ah* 30b).

The mitzvah of *sukkah* is based on Divine law, but there is an ancient custom to adorn the *sukkah* with decorated fabrics, fruits, and grains (*Sukkah* 10a). We should similarly seek to "adorn" the Torah law. We should go beyond the minimum requirements of the Law and aspire to the highest level of God's word, in its purest ethical form. Then we will merit that "David's fallen *sukkah*" (Amos 9:11), the prophet's metaphor for Jewish sovereignty, will rise again, speedily in our days.

A Sukkah of Peace[1]

THE SABBATH EVENING prayers use a peculiar metaphor for peace: וּפְרוֹשׂ עָלֵינוּ סֻכַּת שְׁלוֹמֶךָ – "May You spread over us a *sukkah* of Your peace."

Why pray for a *sukkah*, a makeshift booth, of peace? Would it not be better to have a "fortress of peace" – strong, secure, and lasting?

✦ EVEN IMPERFECT PEACE

Jewish law validates a *sukkah* even when it has gaping holes, when it is built from little more than two walls, or has large spaces between the walls and the roof. Even such a fragile structure still qualifies as a kosher *sukkah*.

The same is true regarding peace. Peace is so precious, so vital, that even if we are unable to attain complete peace, we should still pursue a partial measure of peace. Even an imperfect peace between neighbors, or between an individual and the community, is worthwhile.

"How great is peace!" proclaimed the Sages (*VaYikra Rabbah* 9:9). The value of peace is so great that we pray for it even if it will be like a *sukkah* – flimsy and temporary, rendered fit only by special laws.

---

1 Adapted from *Mo'adei HaRe'iyah*, p. 97.

Succoth and the Land of Israel[1]

In 1907, Rav Kook wrote a Halachic treatise entitled Eitz Hadar, discussing the etrogim grown in Eretz Yisrael and the importance of avoiding grafted etrogim. He advocated the use of etrogim in Eretz Yisrael as a way for world Jewry to strengthen its connection to the land of Israel and support its fledgling communities.

✒ UNDERLYING CONNECTIONS

Our world is an *alma d'peruda*, a reality split into conflicting realms: physical and spiritual, secular and holy, that of compassion and that of strict justice. Yet there always exists a hidden connection that unites these divisions, some intermediary stage or shared level that combines both aspects. This principle is set down by the Torah's esoteric teachings and is confirmed by our own examination of the world around us.

This fundamental truth provides a comprehensive view of the world and gives us insight into the universe's underlying unity.

---

[1]   Adapted from the introduction to *Eitz Hadar*.

✌ TWO CATEGORIES OF MITZVOT

For example, the Sages noted in *Kiddushin* 36b that all mitzvot fall into two categories. The first category consists of מִצְוֹת הַתְּלוּיוֹת בָּאָרֶץ, mitzvot that can only be fulfilled in the land of Israel, such as *Shemitah* (the Sabbatical year) and *ma'aserot* (tithing of fruits and vegetables). The second category consists of those mitzvot that are incumbent even outside of Israel, such as prayer and Torah study. What binds and unites these two types of mitzvot?

We may discern the inner connection between them from the words of the Ramban[2] in his commentary to Gen. 26:5 and Deut. 11:18. The Ramban explained that the root of *all* mitzvot – even those that are incumbent outside of Israel – is in the land of Israel. Performance of mitzvot outside the Land does not fulfill their inner purpose, but rather is a means to enable the Jewish people to return to their land. These mitzvot guard over the holiness of the Jewish people, so that when they return to *Eretz Yisrael* they will not need to re-invent their culture and spiritual path. They will not return to the land of Israel as a young nation, newly arrived on the stage of history, but will continue their ancient traditions. This bold idea is already found in the *Sifre* on Deut. 11:18:

> Even though I exile you from the Land, distinguish yourself with mitzvot.
> Then they will not be new to you when you return [to the land of Israel].

From here we see that both categories of mitzvot share a common dimension, one that is connected to the land of Israel.

In the material world, the most basic form of wealth is real estate. "One who does not possess land is not a person" (*Yevamot* 63a). This is even more evident with regard to nations. Even if a nation expresses itself in higher realms – culture, arts and sciences, and so on – it still requires a fundamental basis in land and agriculture. Land may be compared to the roots of a great tree. Without the beauty of its branches and fruit, the tree is just an ugly

---

2   Rabbi Moses ben Nachman (Nachmanides, 1194–1270), leading Talmudist and Biblical commentator.

stump. "Agriculture," the Sages noted, "is the lowliest form of work" (ibid.). Nonetheless, these roots give life to the entire tree; they are the foundation for all of its produce and beauty.

This idea also holds true in the spiritual realm. All mitzvot share a common denominator – mitzvah-performance in the land of Israel. Thus even our spiritual riches are rooted in the dimension of land.

✺ THE FOUR SPECIES

But is there a specific mitzvah that combines and unites aspects of both categories of mitzvot? To find a mitzvah that bridges these two categories, we will need a mitzvah that, on one hand, is a personal obligation, incumbent also on those not living in Israel; on the other hand, it should be clearly connected to the land of Israel, so that the special qualities of *Eretz Yisrael* are recognizable in it.

The mitzvah of the Four Species (*arba'ah minim*) is a perfect match for these criteria. It is obligatory on every individual, even outside of Israel. At the same time, the Four Species remind us of *Eretz Yisrael* and the harvest, its foliage and beautiful fruit. "Take for yourself a fruit of the citron tree, a palm frond, myrtle branches, and willows of the brook" (Lev. 23:40).

✺ SUCCOTH AND THE LAND OF ISRAEL

In fact, the holiday of Succoth as a whole is integrally connected to the sanctity of the land of Israel and our joy in its fruit. The Sages ruled that an extra month may be added to the year to ensure that Succoth will fall out during the harvest season (*Sifre* 192).

The connection of the Succoth holiday to *Eretz Yisrael* is especially strong in the *etrog* fruit. In the land of Israel it is easy to fulfill this holy mitzvah with joy and beauty. Maimonides suggested that one reason that the Torah chose this particular fruit was its wide availability in *Eretz Yisrael* (*Guide to the Perplexed* 3:43).

In the Diaspora, however, this mitzvah can be difficult and costly. The great effort and expense to attain *etrogim* in the cold and distant lands of our exile reminds us of the desirability of our beloved homeland, a land that suits the special qualities of our soul. When Rabbi Yochanan ben Zakkai instituted special decrees to commemorate the Temple after its destruction, he specifically chose the mitzvah of the Four Species, extending its performance from one day to seven to emulate the way it was performed in the Temple (*Rosh Hashanah* 30a). It is due to this special connection to *Eretz Yisrael* that great scholars throughout the generations went to great lengths to acquire an *etrog* grown in the land of Israel.

❧ *ETROGIM* AND SETTLING THE LAND

In recent years it has been exposed that the vast majority of *etrogim* grown outside of Israel come from lemon trees grafted with *etrog* branches. These grafted *etrogim*, despite their superficial beauty, are not fit for fulfilling the mitzvah of *arba'ah minim*.

In our days, the kosher *etrog* has become another way for us to express our love for the land of Israel. The agricultural settlements in Israel now provide *etrogim* that are supervised to ensure they do not come from grafted trees. It is providential that we should be best able to fulfill this precious mitzvah, connected to the holiday closely bound to the land of Israel, by favoring the produce of the Holy Land. Additionally, as more *etrogim* of *Eretz Yisrael* are purchased, our fellow Jews working the land will be able to plant new orchards. Thus, by buying *etrogim* from Israel, we can all share in the mitzvah of building and settling the land of Israel – a mitzvah on par with the entire Torah (*Sifre Re'eih, Tosefta Avodah Zarah* 5:2).

The Water-Drawing Celebration[1]

URING THE EVENINGS of the Succoth holiday, there was music, dancing, and even juggling in the holy Temple. This joyous activity was called the *Simchat Beit HaSho'eivah*, the Water-Drawing Celebration. While it was usually wine that was used in libation ceremonies, during the holiday of Succoth the *kohanim* poured water – drawn the previous night from Jerusalem's Shiloach spring – next to the altar. This water-offering alludes to the Heavenly judgment for rain that takes place on Succoth.

Yet the nature of these evening celebrations is peculiar. They are called *Simchat Beit HaSho'eivah*, from the word *sho'eivah* meaning "to draw water." This term indicates that the celebrations were not in honor of the actual mitzvah of pouring water on the Temple altar, but rather for the preparatory act of drawing out water from the spring. This appears quite illogical. Why did the people dance and rejoice during the nighttime preparations, and not during the actual Temple service that took place the following day?

---

1 Adapted from *Mo'adei HaRe'iyah*, p. 110. See also *Orot HaTeshuvah* 6:7 (adapted in *Gold from the Land of Israel*, pp. 21–22).

✣ MEANS AND ENDS

In fact, the Water-Drawing Celebration teaches us an important lesson. Generally speaking, we can divide up life's activities into two categories: means and ends. We naturally distinguish between their relative importance, and look upon means as merely a prerequisite to attain a desired goal, but lacking any intrinsic value.

This divide between means and ends goes back to the very beginnings of creation. God commanded the earth to produce "fruit trees that make fruit" (Gen. 1:11). Not only were the trees to produce fruit, but they themselves were to be "fruit trees" – the trees themselves were meant to taste like their fruit. However, the earth failed to bring forth "fruit trees that make fruit"; it only produced "trees that make fruit" – trees that bear fruit, but lack any taste of their own. Why does it matter that our fruit trees are tasteless?

This Midrash refers to this failure as the "Sin of the Earth," and it reflects a basic defect in the universe. The original ideal was that even within the means (the "tree") one would be able to sense the same level of purpose and importance as the final goal (the "fruit"). Unfortunately, this ideal was beyond the world's limited reality. The earth could only bring forth trees that bear fruit, but the trees themselves lack the flavor of their fruit.

✣ ELEVATING THE MEANS

While our current reality makes a sharp distinction between means and ends, nonetheless this original ideal was not completely lost to us. When we sanctify our actions and perform them altruistically, with a pure motive to fulfill God's Will, then even that which only facilitates a mitzvah is elevated to the level of the final goal. At this level of intent, even our preparations have a "taste" of the sweetness and meaningfulness of the mitzvah itself. So it was with the *Simchat Beit HaSho'eivah* celebrations: even in the preparatory act of drawing the water, one could sense the joy and holiness of the actual mitzvah of offering the water on the Temple altar.

Connecting the Natural with the Supernatural[1]

SUCCOTH AND WATER

The highlight of the Temple service during the Succoth holiday was *Nisuch HaMayim*, the Water Libation ceremony. While it was usually wine that was poured at the base of the altar, there is an oral tradition to offer a special libation of water on Succoth.

The Sages (*Shabbat* 103b) found an allusion to this tradition in the verses describing the Succoth offerings (Num. 29:12–34). Three verses conclude with the letters *mem, yud,* and *mem* – spelling out the word *mayim*, water.

What is the special significance of water to the holiday of Succoth? And why does the Torah only hint about the water libation and not mention it explicitly?

FESTIVAL OF HARVEST, FESTIVAL OF BOOTHS

We find two basic themes associated with the Succoth holiday. On the one hand, Succoth is called *Chag Ha'Asif,* the Harvest Festival. Harvesting is the culmination of the entire farming process – starting with plowing, planting, irrigating, and so on, until the crops are ready to be harvested.

1   Adapted from *Ein Ayah* vol. IV on *Shabbat* 103b (12:1).

IOI

Furthermore, harvesting thoroughly involves the natural world. All of the processes of nature must be functioning properly in order that the fruits and grains will be ripe for harvest. Succoth as the Harvest Festival symbolizes the natural world at its most cultivated and completed state.

On the other hand, Succoth is also called the Festival of Booths. Our *sukkah*-huts during the holiday commemorate the miraculous forty-year journey of the Israelites through the desert. During those forty years, the Jewish people were sustained by continuous supernatural phenomena: manna from heaven, Miriam's miraculous well of water, the protective Clouds of God's Presence, and so on.

Why is Succoth associated with two opposing themes: the natural order and the harvest on the one hand, and the supernatural realm of Divine providence and the miraculous trek in the wilderness on the other?

✺ BRIDGING TWO REALMS

In fact, bridging these two themes is the very essence of the Succoth holiday. Succoth is a link between the physical and the metaphysical. It connects the natural world, as epitomized by the autumn harvest, with the realm of Divine intervention, unveiled with the appearance of Israel on the stage of history.

The passage of the Jewish people, from the miraculous Exodus from Egypt to the settlement and everyday life in the land of Israel, bound together the realms of the natural and the supernatural. This bridge revealed the inner connection between a Divinely-created world, designed for the elevated goal of providential justice, and a finished world bound by the fixed laws of science and nature.

✺ WATERS OF CREATION

How does this explain the special connection between water and Succoth? Water recalls the very beginning of creation. The Torah describes the initial stage of creation as "God's spirit hovering over the water" (Gen. 1:2). Even at that primordial state, before the appearance of dry land, God's infinite wisdom set in place all that was needed in order to bring creation to its ultimate form. Thus water reminds us of the Divine wisdom that resides in the very foundations of the world.

In summary, the two themes of Succoth bind together the world's physical nature with its metaphysical essence. This Divine essence was revealed in the emergence of the people of Israel – in the miracles of the Exodus and the journey through the desert – but, in fact, it goes back to the very foundations of the universe. Since the secrets of creation are beyond our grasp, the Torah only alludes to these waters of creation in the final letters of the verses describing the Succoth offerings.

The Role of the Lowly Willow[1]

YOU HAVE TO feel sorry for the poor *aravah*, the willow branch waved together with the other three species of the *arba'ah minim* on Succoth. It lacks the fragrance of the *etrog* and the myrtle, and, unlike the date-palm, it has no fruit. The willow has come to represent the simple folk who are neither learned in Torah nor respected for numerous good deeds.

And yet, according to an ancient oral tradition, the *aravah* becomes the star of the show on Hoshanah Rabbah, the last day of the Succoth holiday. When the Temple stood in Jerusalem, the *kohanim* would raise tall willow boughs around the altar. In synagogues nowadays, after waving all four species, we set aside the other three species and raise the willow alone. And then, at the end of the *Hoshanah* prayers, the congregants beat the willow on the floor.

Why does the lowly willow merit this special attention? And what is the meaning of the age-old custom of striking the floor with willow branches?

✥ SABBATH DESECRATION IN JAFFA

Rav Kook related the following story one holiday evening in his *sukkah*. The incident took place in Jaffa, where Rav Kook served as chief rabbi from 1904 to 1914. One Shabbat day, a secular photographer came and disturbed

---

1   Adapted from *Mo'adei HaRe'iyah*, pp. 111–113.

the Sabbath peace in a religious neighborhood. In total disregard for the local religious sensibilities, he set up his tripod and camera in the middle of the street and began taking pictures.

This public desecration of the Sabbath deeply angered the local residents. One man who was particularly incensed by the photographer's insensitivity took a pail of water and thoroughly soaked the Sabbath-desecrater. Naturally, the photographer was indignant. He was so confident in the justice of his cause that he registered a complaint against the water-douser – at the *beit din* (religious court) of the rabbi of Jaffa, Rav Kook.

Rav Kook told the photographer, "I see that you fail to understand the severity of desecrating the Sabbath in public, but you should realize that your action was a serious affront to the community. You entered a neighborhood of Sabbath-observers and offended them deeply.

"Or course, the correct course of action for the residents would have been to rebuke you verbally. Perhaps you would have understood the seriousness of your actions and stopped. Had that man consulted with me first, I would have advised him not to throw water on you.

"However, he didn't ask, but reacted spontaneously. You should know that on occasion, such impulsive reactions are justified. When people disregard societal norms and cross accepted boundaries, regardless of the implications for others, it is often the spontaneous reaction that most effectively prevents future abuse.

"Such an occasion took place when the Israelites were in the desert and Pinchas responded, not accordingly to the normative Halachah, but as a zealot: *"Kena'im pogim bo"* ("Zealots punish them" – Num. 25:6–8; *Sanhedrin* 82a). If Pinchas had asked beforehand, he would have been instructed not to kill Zimri. But since his act was done sincerely and served to prevent future violations, his zealous deed was approved after the fact."

✜ THE BOETHUSIANS AND THE WILLOW

What about the willow and Succoth? Rav Kook continued his explanation that evening:

The lowly willow represents the common folk, unlearned and lacking exceptional deeds. Yet, these "willows" are blessed with an abundance of common sense and are unencumbered by sophisticated calculations. As a result, they have filled important roles in the history of the Jewish people.

In Talmudic times, there was a sect called the Boethusians who disagreed with many of the rulings of the Sages. One disagreement concerned the willow ceremony. The Boethusians prohibited observing this ceremony on the Sabbath. One year, when Hoshanah Rabbah fell on the Sabbath, the Boethusians took the willows and covered them with stones. They knew the Rabbis would not permit moving the stones on the Sabbath since stones are *muktzeh*.[2]

On Shabbat morning, however, some simple folk who were ignorant about the prohibition of *muktzeh* pulled out the willow boughs from under the stones. Then the *kohanim* were able to raise the willows alongside the altar (*Sukkah* 43b).

Why does the Talmud emphasize that this praiseworthy act was performed by common folk? By covering the boughs with stones, the Boethusians had placed the Sages in a quandary. If the willow boughs were not used, the Boethusians could cite this as proof that the rabbis had conceded to their opinion that willows should not be raised on the Sabbath. On the other hand, if the rabbis decided to move the stones, the Boethusians could have announced that the rabbinic prohibition of *muktzeh* had been abolished.

Fortunately, the problem never materialized. The simple Jews resolved the dilemma in their own typical manner. They did not ask questions; rather, alarmed by the scandal, they responded by simply removing the willows from under the stones.

ɞ THE ROLE OF THE WILLOW

The custom to hit the floor with willows does not mean that we wish to "punish" the willow, as is often thought, for its lack of Torah and good deeds. Rather, it is meant to demonstrate that the willow is also a force to be reckoned with – a natural, healthy power that is part of the arsenal of the Jewish people. We do not strike the willow. We strike *with* the willow.

---

2 *Muktzeh* refers to various categories of objects (stones, money, work tools, etc.) that the Rabbis prohibited to be handled on the Sabbath in order to safeguard the sanctity of the day.

CHANUKAH
חנוכה

The Pure Vessel of Inner Faith

In every Jew there resides an aspect of *kehunah* [priesthood], since together they form "a kingdom of *kohanim* and a holy nation" (Ex. 19:6). Hidden in the depths of the Jewish heart is an inner drive for a life of holiness and Torah wisdom. . . . And the small cruse of oil – [representing] this hidden inner realm – sealed with the mark of the High Priest, could not be contaminated by the Greeks.

At that hour, a time of upheaval and confusion, when the Hellenist lifestyle spread throughout the land of Israel, only the inner faith that dwells in the depths of the heart remained intact. This is the metaphor of the cruse that was found – a cruse of pure oil, sealed with the mark of the high priesthood.

(*Mo'adei HaRe'iyah*, p. 166)

The Hellenist Challenge[1]

WHEN THE GREEKS entered the Temple, they defiled all of the oils. After the Hasmoneans defeated them, they searched and found but one cruse of oil, untouched and sealed with the seal of the High Priest. The cruse had only enough oil for one day, but a miracle occurred and they were able to light from it for eight days. The following year they established these days as a holiday for praise and thanksgiving. (*Shabbat* 21b)

We may ask a number of questions on the Talmudic account of Chanukah:

The Jewish people have fought many battles in their long history. Some of these battles were accompanied by miracles, such as the walls of Jericho that fell and the sun that stood still during the battle at Givon. Why was only the Hasmonean victory chosen to be commemorated as a holiday for future generations?

Why celebrate a military conflict in which the Temple was defiled and many Jews were lost to a foreign culture?

Why is there no mitzvah to celebrate Chanukah with a festive meal, unlike other holidays? Why only "a holiday of praise and thanksgiving"?

---

1   Adapted from *Ein Ayah* vol. III on *Shabbat* 21b (2:13).

What is the significance of the miracle of the undefiled cruse of oil?

❧ CULTURE CLASH

The military victories of the Greek empire brought about the spread of Greek culture and philosophy, and the superficial charm of Hellenism captured the hearts of many Jews. These new ideas undermined fundamental teachings of the Torah and central mitzvot. The danger was so great that this clash of cultures could have caused permanent damage to the spiritual state of the Jewish people.

The Talmud emphasizes the significance of the small cruse of oil in the rescue of the Jewish people. The sealed jar of pure oil is a metaphor for the kernel of pure faith that resides in the depths of the Jewish soul. It was this inner resource of pure holiness that guarded the Jewish people in their struggle against Hellenism.

The Sages understood that Chanukah needed to be established as a permanent holiday. They realized that the battle against an overwhelming foreign culture was not just the one-time struggle of the Hasmoneans. All generations require the strength and purity of inner faith to protect the Torah from the corrupting influences of foreign beliefs and values.

❧ THE CONTRIBUTION OF HELLENISM

The Sages also realized that this conflict with Hellenism, despite its disastrous short-term effects, would ultimately bestow great benefits. This is a basic rule of life: those challenges that confront us and threaten our beliefs and way of life will in the end invigorate the sources of truth. Greek wisdom, after it has acknowledged the Divine nature of Torah, will serve to further honor and strengthen the Torah and its ideals. Therefore it is fitting to celebrate these days, despite the trauma of the Hasmonean period.

Significantly, the festival of Chanukah is celebrated without feasting and wine. There were two sides to Hellenism: its intellectual aspects – Greek philosophy, literature, and so on – and its popular culture of physical pleasures and crass entertainment. One might mistakenly think that Hellenism's positive contribution also includes its hedonistic delight in wine, parties, and naked wrestling matches. Therefore we specifically celebrate Chanukah with spiritual rituals – lights and *Hallel*, praise and thanksgiving. For the true contribution of Hellenism is its intellectual side, that which posed such a grave challenge to the Torah in the times of the Hasmoneans. It is this aspect of Greek culture that will defend and enhance the Torah in the future.

॰ꙮ

Flickering Lights in Dark Times[1]

॰ꙮ SUITABLE WICKS AND OILS

The Mishnah (*Shabbat*, chapter two) discusses which wicks and oils are suitable for Sabbath lights. Certain materials may not be used for wicks since they make "the flame sputter" and fail to burn evenly; and certain oils may not be used because "they do not flow freely to the wick." With regard to Chanukah, however, the Talmud (*Shabbat* 21b) rules that these restrictions do not apply. Even wicks and oil that do not burn smoothly may be used for Chanukah lights. Why are all oils permitted for use on Chanukah, even when lit on Friday evening? Why this distinction between Sabbath and Chanukah lights?

The Sages required that Sabbath lights be lit from high-quality oils and wicks in order to prevent situations where one might be tempted to relight or adjust sputtering lights (and thus desecrate the Sabbath). They were more lenient, however, regarding Chanukah, since Chanukah lights need not be re-lit should the flame go out. Also, since it is forbidden to use their light for reading or other purposes, the Sages were less concerned that one would attempt to relight a poorly-lit Chanukah light.

---

1   Adapted from *Ein Ayah* vol. III on *Shabbat* 21b (2:5).

❧ THE LIGHTS OF CHANUKAH

Rav Kook explained that the special rules of Chanukah lights reflect the nature of the Maccabean struggle against Greek dominance, in both political and cultural spheres.

The authentic heritage of Israel is Torah. The Torah's eternal wisdom is symbolized by the Sabbath lights – lights that require a pure oil that burns clearly and brightly.

However, there have been many times during their long history when the Jewish people have been attracted to the wisdom and beliefs of other nations. This phenomenon is particularly prevalent when the Jewish people are ruled by other nations or exiled from their land. During these times of national vulnerability, many are drawn to the ideologies of powerful and successful nations, even if these beliefs are not thoroughly considered and may be based only on theories and speculations.

For such times, Divine providence provided the Jewish people with gifted scholars who were able to defend the Torah by utilizing these foreign ideas. One example is Maimonides, who attempted where possible to reconcile Aristotelian philosophy with the Torah.

❧ SHORT-LIVED FLAME

However, these foreign philosophies lack the eternal truth of Torah. They are like flickering flames that illuminate only for a short time. After a generation or two, the assumptions upon which these ideas are based are often refuted. Utilizing foreign philosophies to bolster the Torah may be compared to lighting Chanukah lights with oils that fail to produce a bright and even light.

Nonetheless, when these beliefs are popular and widely-held, the generation is strongly drawn to them. If it were not possible to find some measure of agreement with the Torah, many would be tempted to reject the Torah altogether. In order to protect the nation, Divine providence allowed the possibility of aligning these fashionable ideas with the Torah's wisdom. They do not always match neatly with practical mitzvot and Halachic rulings – in the words of the Talmud, "they do not flow freely to the wick" – but with a little effort, they can be made to at least partially correspond.

We should be aware that such philosophies are not eternal truths and we are not responsible for their accuracy. "When their light goes out, they need not be re-lit." Certainly we should not make practical changes to Torah observance based on these ideas – "it is forbidden to make use of its light." They are useful only to put troubled minds to rest, not as a true foundation with practical implications. Thus the special rules of Chanukah lights aptly parallel the Maccabean struggle against the Greeks, at a time when Hellenism and Greek wisdom dominated the world with its new ideas.

❧ JEWISH NATIONALISM

There was a second arena in which the Maccabees contested the Greek empire: the military-political one. Here too, the Hasmonean rule did not follow the eternal path of Israel, which designated the monarchy to the descendants of David for all generations. The throne of David is compared to an eternal flame – "You promised him that his candle will never be extinguished" (from the Sabbath prayers). But the hour was not ripe for a Davidic king, and the temporary rule of the Hasmoneans provided stability and independence for many years.

The Davidic dynasty combined both Torah scholarship and political leadership. David studied Torah assiduously day and night (*Berachot* 3b), and at the same time was energetic and decisive in establishing a secure reign. Authentic Jewish nationalism must be based on the light of Torah – "From Zion, Torah will come forth" (Isaiah 2:3).

In summary, the laws of Chanukah lights reflect the transient quality of the Hasmonean victory, both spiritually and materially. Spiritually – the accommodation of foreign philosophies that may be partially reconciled with the Torah's teachings, as represented by oils that do not burn well. And materially – a political rule not of the Davidic dynasty. This corresponds to the wicks (the more material side of the lights) that fail to hold a constant flame. These achievements provided light, albeit a weak and unsteady one, for a people lacking true independence. They are only fit for Chanukah lights, commemorating a holiday that was not inscribed for all generations in the Biblical canon (*Yoma* 29a). Yet even though they are not the ideal, unlike the pure lights of the Sabbath, we need these lights during the precarious times of foreign occupation and exile.

‰ *KODESH HEIM*

Despite their shortcomings, these transient lights are holy – "*kodesh heim*." We should recognize in them the hand of God, that God prepared a path so that those attracted to the prevalent culture should not be lost. And the very fact that foreign ideas may be accommodated within the Torah is an indication that these ideas contain a kernel of eternal truth – a small cruse of pure oil, sealed with the stamp of High Priest.

Richness of Spirit[1]

<hr />

THE HOLIDAY OF Chanukah raises a number of questions:

Why do we celebrate Chanukah for eight days? After all, there was enough oil to burn for one day, so the miracle was really only for seven days. Since the holiday commemorates the miracle of the oil, we should celebrate for only seven days.[2]

The minimum requirement is for each family to light one candle each night. It is customary, however, is to light with two *hiddurim* (embellishments): every member of the family lights, and the number of candles corresponds to the day of Chanukah. Why do we perform these two *hiddurim*?

The Talmud in *Menachot* 28b relates that the Maccabees were unable to obtain a solid gold Menorah for the Temple as the Torah specifies. Lacking the means for such an expensive Menorah, they constructed a simple one out of iron rods plated with tin. Why was there a miracle for the oil but none for the Menorah itself?

ᎌ TWO *HIDDURIM*

The truth is, had the Maccabees not found the small cruse of pure olive

<hr />

1   Adapted from *Igrot HaRe'iyah* vol. III, p. 797.

2   This question was raised by Rabbi Joseph Karo (1488–1575) in his commentary *Beit Yosef* to *Orach Chayim* 670.

oil, they could have used any oil. While it is best to use olive oil, any oil that burns well may be used in the Temple Menorah.

The miracle of Chanukah could have been the Menorah burning all eight days with "miracle oil." But while "miracle oil" is as good as any other oil, it is not olive oil. Thus the miracle of the first day of Chanukah was not the burning of "miracle oil," but that the Maccabees found ritually pure olive oil. This discovery was quite unexpected, and it enabled them to light with the optimal type of oil.

In addition, since the majority of the nation at the time was ritually impure, the Maccabees could even have used impure oil. The miracle of finding the cruse of olive oil thus allowed them to fulfill two *hiddurim*: lighting on the first day with olive oil, and lighting with ritually pure oil. We commemorate this miracle by similarly performing two *hiddurim*, with every family member lighting, and lighting multiple candles.

֍ GUARDING THE INNER SPIRIT

But why was there no comparable miracle with the Menorah itself? Why didn't the Maccabees also find a gold Menorah in the desecrated Temple?

The Menorah corresponds to the material state of the Jewish people. It is a vessel for holding the oil. The olive oil, on the other hand, is a metaphor for the nation's inner spirit.

While it is fitting that the external vessel should be aesthetically pleasing, there are times when the physical reality is harsh and discouraging. During such times, we make do with what we have, even if it means lighting with a Menorah improvised out of iron rods.

However, the spirit – the oil that nourishes the inner flame – must always remain spiritually rich, with all of the *hiddurim* of purity and holiness. This is an important part of the message of Chanukah: the miracle occurred, not with the Menorah, but with the oil. We may suffer physical hardships and deprivation, but our inner spiritual life should always shine with a clear and pure light.

The Single Light of Chanukah[1]

EFORE LIGHTING THE Chanukah lights, we recite the blessing, "Who sanctified us with His mitzvot and commanded us to kindle the Chanukah light." Why does the blessing refer to a single light – "the Chanukah light"? We light several candles each night; why not say "the Chanukah *lights*"?

✷ CHANUKAH AND CHINUCH

The word *Chanukah* means "dedication," referring to the re-dedication of the Temple after its desecration by the Seleucid emperor Antiochus IV. *Chanukah* shares the same Hebrew root as *chinuch* – "education." But *chinuch* is the masculine form of the word while *chanukah* is the feminine form. Why?

Rav Kook explained that the goal of education is to nurture the student to grow and develop by inculcating good habits and proper conduct. Education develops their innate talents and natural integrity, and has a positive influence over the years to come. Therefore the word *chinuch* is in the

---

1   Adapted from *Olat Re'iyah* vol. I, pp. 433–435.

masculine form, as it indicates a process of striving and developing inner potential.[2]

The dedication of the Temple, however, was a greatly different situation. From when it was first established, the Temple already encompassed all of its greatness and holiness. Future times will merely reveal the holiness that it always contained. Thus the Temple's dedication is called *chanukah*. The feminine form of the word is used, denoting a state of intrinsic holiness and completeness.

THE LIGHTS OF ISRAEL

The lights of Chanukah are a metaphor for the blessings of enlightenment that the Jewish people bestow to the world. All of the nation's potential spiritual gifts are included in the dedication of Chanukah: Torah and wisdom, prophecy and morality, justice and compassion, and so on. Like the Temple, these are qualities inherent in the people of Israel – so the word *chanukah* is appropriate.

Sometimes these "lights" emphasize their distinct nature in order to make their full contribution, even at the expense of other ideals. Such divisions, however, can lead to internal strife. Those who stress one particular ideal may look upon those who promote other ideals as detracting from a more important value. In truth, when each individual advances that light that corresponds to the inner makeup of his soul, the entire people of Israel is enriched.

But these conflicts will not exist forever. As long as there is strife and dissension, holiness cannot be properly established. In the future it will become clear that all of the different lights share a common root, and are really one single light. Therefore, the blessing of Chanukah, which also encompasses the future potential, speaks of a single "Chanukah light."

---

2   The Kabbalists described the active *sephirot* (spiritual vessels for revealing God's infinite light in the world) as "masculine," and the passive or receptive *sephirot* as "feminine."

※

The Highest Love[1]

I

S THERE SOMETHING idealistic and holy in loving the Jewish people? Or is this just another form of nationalism, an emotion far less noble than a universal love for all peoples?

﹛ CHANUKAH LIGHTS

The minimal obligation during Chanukah is to light one candle each night of the holiday. The academies of Hillel and Shamai, however, disagreed as to the optimal way to light:

> The school of Shamai ruled that the most punctilious individuals (*Mehadrin min HaMehadrin*) light eight lights on the first day, and the number of lights decreases each day. But the school of Hillel ruled that they should light one light on the first day, and the number of lights increases with each passing day. (*Shabbat* 21b)

What is the reasoning behind each opinion? The Talmud explains that Beit Shamai compared the Chanukah lights to the bull offerings on Succoth, which decrease in number on each successive day of the holiday. Beit Hillel,

---

1   Adapted from *Ein Ayah* vol. III on *Shabbat* 21b (2:7).

on the hand, followed the dictum that "In holy matters, one should increase and not detract."

Is there a deeper philosophical basis for this disagreement? And what is the connection between Chanukah and the Succoth offerings?

✣ THE JEWISH HOME

The conflict between the Maccabees and the Hellenists was not just a military struggle for political independence. The essence of the conflict was ideological, a clash between widely divergent cultures. Greek culture emphasized the joys of life, physical pleasures, and the uninhibited expression of human imagination in art and literature. As a result, the Hellenists fought against the Torah of Israel, with its focus on purity and sanctity.

One aspect of the mitzvah of lighting Chanukah lights is quite unusual. Unlike most mitzvot, the obligation to light is not on the individual but on the home ("*ish uveito*"). Only if one wishes to fulfill the mitzvah more fully does every member of the household light. Why is this?

The average Jew may not exemplify the ideals and beliefs of the Torah in his everyday life. But in his family life, one may sense the special light of Israel. Purity, modesty, and other holy traits are manifest in every Jewish home faithful to a Torah lifestyle. Therefore, the basic obligation of Chanukah lights – which represent Judaism's victory over the corrupting influences of Greek culture – is not on the individual, but the home: "*ish uveito.*"

✣ THE *MEHADRIN*

There are, however, righteous individuals whose personal life does in fact exemplify the sanctity of Torah. They are suitable to be *Mehadrin*, each one lighting his own Chanukah light, since the light of Torah accompanies them in all of their actions. It is about these holy individuals and the spiritual light they project that the Torah writes, "And all the peoples of the world will realize that God's Name is called upon you and they will be in awe of you" (Deut. 28:10).

Finally, there is a third level, even higher – the *Mehadrin min HaMehadrin*.

These are selfless individuals whose efforts are not for their own personal welfare, not even for their own spiritual elevation. Rather, they aspire to fulfill God's Will in the world. The miracle of Chanukah inspires these elevated individuals to pursue their lofty goal, and they light accordingly, increasing (or decreasing, according to Beit Shamai) the number of lights each day.

৯৹ THE UNIVERSALISTIC APPROACH

Yet we may ask: what is God's Will? What is the ultimate goal of creation? This question is at the heart of the disagreement between the schools of Hillel and Shamai.

The *Mehadrin min HaMehadrin* may follow one of two paths. The first is to meditate on God's Will by considering the multitudes of peoples and nations that God created. For what purpose did God create all of these souls stamped in His Divine image? Surely God intended that ultimately they will be elevated, raised from the depths of ignorance and brought to the level of the righteous who delight in God and His goodness.

According to this view, the mission of the Jewish people is to inspire all nations to strive for Divine enlightenment and a life of holiness. The ultimate purpose in keeping the Torah and its mitzvot is not to elevate the Jewish people, but for the more universal goal of benefiting all of humanity. The focus of one's life should not be love of one's people but love of God and His Torah, for the Torah encompasses the true goal of elevating all of humanity, and love of Israel is merely a means to this end.

৯৹ LOVE FOR THE NATION

The second approach agrees that any form of self-love is unsuitable to be one's highest goal, even if it is love of one's own people. Rather, we should love that which is good for its own sake. We should strive to advance that which is the highest and loftiest. Since the Jewish people are blessed with a special *segulah*, an intrinsic quality of holiness, they have the potential to attain the highest state, and they will remain the focus of all spiritual life even after the elevation of the other nations of the world.

Love of Israel is thus a true value of Torah, since the ultimate goal will always be the elevation of Israel. The purpose of creation is not measured in quantity but in quality, and the Jewish people will always retain a unique advantage due to their *segulah* quality.

THE SCHOOL OF SHAMAI

How do these two approaches relate to the disagreement between Beit Hillel and Beit Shamai?

The universalistic outlook sees Israel's mission as an agent of change, inspiring all peoples to form a harmonious society living a life of righteousness and sanctity. Over time, the plurality of diverse national characteristics will diminish as they absorb the ever-brighter light of truth. As the nations are drawn to the holiness of Torah, their unique ideologies and traits will become less distinct. This is the approach of Beit Shamai, who taught to progressively reduce the number of Chanukah lights until there remains but a single resplendent light.

This view sees the story of Chanukah as a milestone in a long historical process. The confrontation with Greek culture and the subsequent victory of Israel brought about a greater interaction and influence of Israel upon the nations. The struggle with Hellenism significantly increased the world's familiarity with the Torah's teachings. Thus it is fitting that the lights of Chanukah should reflect the historical process of the world's progressive elevation and unification.

THE OPINION OF BEIT HILLEL

Beit Hillel certainly concurred with this universal mission of the Jewish people. But is Israel merely a tool to elevate the rest of the world? The true goal of the Torah is to establish the highest level of sanctified life possible – and that can only be attained through the intrinsic *segulah* quality of Israel.

While the Jewish people appear to suffer from spiritual decline over time, the inner holiness of Israel can only be properly measured if we take into account all the generations over time. Every generation that affirms Israel's special covenant with God, despite the pressures of persecution and exile, contributes to the overall *segulah* of this unique people.

The many nations of the world are certainly numerically superior. Yet Israel is not just a vehicle for their spiritual elevation. On the contrary, their elevation is a means that facilitates the emergence of a loftier sanctity of Israel. The nations will enable the unique *segulah* that will crown the world in the end of days – an entire people prepared to live life on the highest level of holiness. This is the ultimate goal of the world, as the Sages taught, "The idea of Israel preceded all of creation" (*Breishit Rabbah* 1:4).

How does this outlook see the lights of Chanukah? Despite the importance of the Hasmonean victory and the resulting increase in Israel's influence on the world, the quantitative advance is still secondary in importance to the qualitative goal. Therefore on each night we add an additional Chanukah light, to symbolize the increased light of Israel. The focus is not on the gradual unification and elevation of the nations of the world, but on the increasing light emanating from Israel, as it intensifies in brightness and diversity, reaching out to each nation according to its special characteristics and needs.

We may now better understand the Talmud's explanation for the opinions of Beit Shamai and Beit Hillel. Beit Shamai, who stressed the universalistic aspect of Israel's influence on the world, compared the Chanukah lights to the bull offerings of Succoth. What is special about these offerings? The Sages (*Sukkah* 55b) noted that the total number of bull offerings was seventy. These seventy offerings were brought for the spiritual benefit of the seventy nations of the world.

Beit Hillel, on the other hand, taught that "In holy matters, one should increase and not detract." The reason why love for the Jewish people is an authentic goal of the Torah is due to the special *segulah* of Israel. Its existence is a goal even higher than the elevation of all of humanity. Love of the Jewish people is rightfully considered a holy matter, as it fully appreciates the unique role of Israel in the universe.

﹩ JEWISH NATIONALISM

To question whether Jewish nationalism is a genuine Torah value reveals a superficial knowledge of Torah. The real question is whether the ultimate Divine goal is quantitative – the elevation of all of humanity through Israel and its Torah – or qualitative – the incomparable *segulah* quality of Israel. To use Rabbi Yehudah HaLevi's metaphor of Israel as the "heart among the nations," the disagreement between Beit Hillel and Beit Shamai may be presented as follows: Is the heart subservient to the other organs of the body, as it provides them with life-giving blood? Or is the heart the central organ, protected and sustained by the rest of the body? Both of these positions are legitimate; "Both views are the words of the Living God" (*Eiruvin* 13b).

This is the basis for a true understanding of nationalism in Israel. It transcends the usual form of nationalism as it is found among other nations. This unique national love is based on the ultimate Divine goal that can only be fulfilled through the Jewish people. While Jewish nationalism contains elements common to regular nationalism, it is of a completely different order.

PURIM
פורים

The Elevated Holiness of Purim

In contrast to Yom Kippur, a day without eating and drinking, the sacred eating of the Purim festive meal is higher and more elevated. The obligation to become inebriated (*le-bisumei*) on Purim contains a measure of the sublime fragrance (*bisum*) mentioned as one of the special gifts of the messianic king — "And he will smell [the truth] by [merit of his] awe of God" (Isaiah 11:3).[1]

(*Mo'adei HaRe'iyah*, p. 240; *Olat Re'iyah* vol. 1, p. 437)

---

[1]   The Hebrew name for the Day of Atonement, *Yom Kipurim*, may be read as *Yom Ki-Purim*, a "Day like Purim." This implies that even Yom Kippur, the holiest day of the year, can only approximate the unique holiness of Purim. (Cf. *Tikunei Zohar* 57b: "Purim is called by the name *Yom Ki-Purim*, for in the future they will delight in Yom Kippur, transforming it from affliction to enjoyment.") Unlike Yom Kippur, whose holiness requires that the body be afflicted with fasting, on Purim we are able to serve God even with physical pleasures, in feasting and drinking.

The elevated harmony between body and soul on Purim alludes to the lofty state of the Messianic Era. The messianic king will not need to judge the people using his external senses — "He will not judge with the sight of his eyes, nor will he rebuke with the hearing of his ears" (Isaiah 11:3) — but he will utilize an inner spiritual perception, similar to the sense of smell (*Sanhedrin* 93b).

Parashat Shekalim: All for One[1]

WHEN YOU TAKE a census of the Israelites [to determine] their numbers, each one will be counted by giving an atonement offering for his life. . . . Everyone included in the census must give a half-shekel.

(Ex. 30:12–13)

Why were the Israelites commanded to give a *half*-shekel coin, and not a whole shekel? And why is this donation required when counting the people?

✥ THE UNITY OF ISRAEL

All societies require a degree of harmony and goodwill. Social cohesion is critical to attain prosperity and success. For the Jewish people, however, unity is not just a means to achieve worldly objectives. Social unity is a far greater value, a goal unto itself. Our highest aspiration is to merit closeness to God, and God's Presence dwells in Israel only when they live in peace and harmony. As the Sages taught: "When is My Name called upon Israel? When they are united" (*Sifre VeZot HaBrachah* 346).

There is a second difference between the unity sought by the Jewish people and that of the other nations. A society may be unified in two ways:

---

1 Adapted from *Midbar Shur*, pp. 127–136.

in deed and in thought. "Unity in deed" refers to practical actions to assist one's neighbors or to contribute to the nation as a whole. "Unity in thought" means concern for fellow citizens and love for one's people.

While all nations need both forms of unity, only practical cooperation is essential for a nation to realize its material objectives. For the Jewish people, however, peace is a prerequisite for God's Presence and special providence, and this peace depends primarily on unity in the heart. Thus, for Israel "unity in thought" is the ultimate goal, while "unity in deed" is a means to bolster and strengthen it.

✍ THE MITZVAH OF *SHEKALIM*

What does this have to do with the yearly donation of half-shekels? The collection of half-shekels is a vehicle for uniting the Jewish people in deed and action. The money was used to provide for the nation's spiritual needs – to supply the daily Temple offerings – as well as its material needs – funds left over were used to maintain the city walls and towers (*Shekalim* 4:1–2).

When other nations unite for some public objective, such as raising an army or collecting taxes, they arrange a census in order to determine how much each individual must contribute toward the collective effort. This census does not contradict the purpose of their unified efforts, since the ultimate goal is to benefit each individual.[2] For the Jewish people, however, the purpose of joining together is to benefit and elevate the nation as a whole. A census negates the ultimate objective, as it emphasizes the portion of the individual. For this reason, the Torah requires that we do not count the people directly, but use half-shekel coins donated for national needs, thereby stressing that this count is for the benefit of the nation.

The half-shekel coins collected in the time of Moses were used to make the *adanim*, the silver sockets that formed the Tabernacle's foundation. This act established the connection between each individual's service of God and the spiritual accomplishments of the nation. Even without a spiritual center

---

2   Cf. John Locke's philosophy of government as based on the natural rights of the individual (social contract theory).

in Jerusalem, the unity of Israel protects the Jewish people, as the service of each individual contributes to elevate the nation as a whole.

Directing this benefit to the nation requires some unifying act. This was initially accomplished through the donations to build the Tabernacle. Later it was the half-shekels donated for the daily Temple service. And nowadays it is performed through our communal reading of *Parashat Shekalim* each year.

҂ HAMAN'S SHEKELS

We may now understand what the Sages wrote in *Megillah* 13b:

> God knew that Haman would pay shekel coins for [permission to destroy] the Jews. Therefore God anticipated the shekel coins of the Jewish people to those of Haman, as we learned, "The collection of *shekalim* is announced on the first day of Adar" [thus preceding Haman's plot to annihilate the Jews on the thirteenth of Adar].

What is the connection between our donations and Haman's bribe? The nations were aware of the special Divine providence protecting the Jewish people and were reluctant to harm them. Haman, however, felt that this protection was only in force when the Jewish people lived together as one people in their own land. But once they were exiled from their land, they were no longer a nation, just a group of individuals – "dispersed and separated among the nations" (Esther 3:8). Stripped of their Divine protection, he reasoned that it was now possible to annihilate them. Therefore he weighed out his silver shekels to purchase the right "to destroy them" (Esther 3:9). Not "to destroy *it*" – the nation – but *them* – these dispersed individuals.

God, however, thwarted his plot, as the Jewish people are united even when they are in exile. By preceding Haman's shekels with our shekel donation, we demonstrate the unity and collective holiness of Israel at all times.

THE SECOND HALF-SHEKEL

Each individual was commanded to give a half-shekel in the census. Why a half-shekel? They would have certainly donated a full shekel were it not for the specific instruction that "the wealthy shall not add more." The two halves of the shekel correspond to the two forms of unity. The half-shekel that was given reflects their unity in deed, their practical cooperation; and the second half that they *wanted* to give corresponds to their unity in thought.

The Midrash states that Moses had difficulty understanding which coin to collect, so God showed him a half-shekel coin made out of fire from beneath His Throne of Glory (*Bemidbar Rabbah* 12:3). What did Moses have difficulty understanding? And why does the Midrash speak of a fire-coin that came from beneath God's throne?

Moses did not understand why the Israelites needed to donate a half-shekel and not a full shekel. Therefore God showed him a fire-coin from a very elevated place, from under His throne, the source of the souls of Israel. In other words, God showed Moses the second half of the shekel – not the metal coin that was collected, a sign of their practical cooperation, but a coin of fire, representing their unity in thought, a burning love emanating from the very root of their souls.

Accepting the Torah in the
Days of Ahasuerus[1]

W HY DID THE Sages enjoin us to become inebriated on Purim?

ASSIMILATION IN ANCIENT PERSIA

The Talmud in *Megillah* 12a states that the near-annihilation of the Jews in the time of Ahasuerus was a punishment for participating in the royal banquet, where they prostrated themselves before Persian idols. What led them to this act of disloyalty?

The Jews of that time believed that the root cause of anti-Semitism was due to a xenophobic hatred of their distinct culture and religion. In fact, this was Haman's explanation for seeking to destroy them:

> There is a certain people scattered and dispersed among the peoples in all the provinces of your kingdom. Their laws are different from those of every people; neither do they keep the king's laws. (Esther 3:8)

In order to overcome this hatred, the Jews felt that it would be prudent to adopt the customs and ways of their idolatrous neighbors. They demonstrated their allegiance as loyal Persian subjects by attending the royal banquet and bowing down to the Persian idols.

To their consternation, the Jews soon discovered that their efforts were

---

1   Adapted from *Olat Re'iyah* vol. I, p. 441.

futile. They were shocked to learn of Haman's plot to annihilate them, despite their best attempts at integrating into the local culture.

ACCEPTING THE TORAH AGAIN

With the realization that assimilation is not the answer, and that their only true protection is God's providence, the Jews reaffirmed their commitment to keep the Torah and its mitzvot. This is the meaning of the verse, "They confirmed and accepted upon themselves" (Esther 9:27) – "they confirmed what they had accepted long before" at Mount Sinai (*Shabbat* 88a).

The Talmud teaches that their renewed commitment to Torah complemented and completed the original acceptance of Torah at Sinai. What was missing at Sinai? The dramatic revelation at Mount Sinai contained an element of coercion. Alone and helpless in the wilderness, the Israelites were hardly in a position to refuse. The Midrash portrays this limited free choice with God's threat to bury them beneath the mountain had they refused to accept the Torah. In the time of Ahasuerus, however, they voluntarily accepted the Torah in a spirit of pure free will, thus completing the original acceptance of Torah at Sinai.

EFFUSION OF GOOD WILL

This appears to be the explanation for the unusual rabbinic requirement to become inebriated on Purim (*Megilah* 7b). It is ordinarily forbidden to become drunk, since without the intellect to guide us, our uncontrolled desires may lead us to improper and unbecoming behavior.

But on Purim, the entire Jewish nation was blessed with an outpouring of good will to accept the Torah. On this special day, we find within ourselves a sincere yearning to embrace the Torah and its teachings. For this reason, we demonstrate on Purim that even when intoxicated we do not stray from the path of Torah, since we are naturally predisposed to goodness and closeness to God. Even in a drunken state, we are confident that we will not be shamed or humiliated by the exposure of our innermost desires. As we say in the *Shoshanat Ya'akov* prayer on Purim: "To make known that all who place their hope in You will not be shamed, and all who take refuge in You will never be humiliated."

The Assault of Amalek[1]

AMALEK ATTACKED THE Israelites at Rephidim, intentionally targeting the weak and those lagging behind. Joshua engaged Amalek in battle, successfully defending Israel against this merciless enemy. Then God instructed Moses:

> Write this as a reminder in the book, and recite it in Joshua's ears: I will completely obliterate the memory of Amalek from under the heavens.
>
> (Ex. 17:14)

Why did God command Moses to write down His promise to obliterate Amalek in the Torah? And why did Joshua need to be told verbally? Couldn't Joshua just read what was written in the Torah?

TWO MISSIONS

The Jewish people have two missions. At Mount Sinai, God informed them that they would be a *mamlechet kohanim* ("kingdom of priests") as well as a *goy kadosh* ("holy nation") (Ex. 19:6). What is the difference between these two goals?

Mamlechet kohanim refers to our aspiration to uplift the entire world,

---

1 Adapted from *Midbar Shur*, pp. 312–316.

so that all will recognize God. The people of Israel fulfill this mission when they function as *kohanim* for the world, teaching them God's ways.

But the Jewish people are not just a tool to elevate the rest of the world. They have their own intrinsic value, and they need to perfect themselves on their own special level. The central mission of Israel is to fulfill its spiritual potential and become a *goy kadosh*. If Israel's sole function was to uplift the rest of the world, they would not have been commanded with mitzvot that isolate them from the other nations, such as the laws of *kashrut* and circumcision.

֍ TWO TORAHS

God divided the Torah, our guide to fulfill our spiritual missions, into two components: the Written Law and the Oral Law. The written Torah was revealed to the entire world; all nations can access these teachings. God commanded that the Torah be written "in a clear script" (Deut. 27:8) – in seventy languages, so that it would be accessible to all peoples (*Sotah* 7:5). The Written Torah was meant to enlighten the entire world.

The Oral Law, on the other hand, belongs solely to the Jewish people. Since this part of Torah was not meant to be committed to writing,[2] it is of a more concealed and less universal nature. In truth, the Oral Law is simply the received explanation of the Written Law, transmitted over the generations. Thus even the Written Torah is only fully accessible to Israel through the Oral Torah. But the other nations nevertheless merit a limited understanding of the Written Torah.

֍ GOD'S NAME AND THRONE

Amalek rejected both missions of Israel. Amalek cannot accept Israel as a *mamlechet kohanim* instructing the world, nor as a *goy kadosh*, separate from

---

2   It is forbidden to commit the Oral Law to writing (*Gittin* 60b). This prohibition was relaxed by Rabbi Yehudah HaNasi in the second century when he wrote down the Mishnah out of concern that the integrity of the Oral Law would be lost due to the exile and dispersion of the Jewish people (Maimonides, introduction to *Mishneh Torah*).

the other nations with its own unique spiritual aspirations. God promised to "completely obliterate" (*macho emcheh*) Amalek. In Hebrew, the verb is repeated, indicating that God will blot out both aspects of Amalek's rejection of Israel.

Why did God command that His promise to destroy Amalek be written down and also transmitted orally? Since Amalek rejects Israel's mission to elevate humanity, God commanded that His promise to obliterate Amalek be recorded in the Written Torah. The Written Law is, after all, the primary source of Israel's moral influence on the world. And since Amalek also denies Israel's unique spiritual heritage, God commanded that this promise be transmitted verbally, corresponding to the Oral Law, the exclusive Torah of Israel.

When Amalek has been utterly destroyed, the Jewish nation will be able to fulfill both of its missions. This is the significance of the statement of the Sages:

> God vowed that His Name and His Throne are not complete until Amalek's name will be totally obliterated.
>
> (*Tanchuma Ki Tetzei* 11; Rashi on Ex. 17:16)

What are "God's Name" and "God's Throne"? They are metaphors for Israel's two missions: spreading knowledge of God – His Name – and creating a special dwelling place for God's Presence in the world – His Throne. Amalek and its obstructionist worldview must be eradicated before these two goals can be accomplished.

Wine Enters, Secrets Emerge[1]

W HAT IS THE significance of the Talmudic instruction to drink on the holiday of Purim?

The Sages taught, "Wine enters, and secrets emerge" (*Eiruvin* 65a). In our generation, we very much need our inner secrets to come out and be revealed. Through this revelation, we will discover that which is hidden in our souls and learn to recognize our true selves.

When we reach the level of intoxication prescribed by the Sages – "*ad d'lo yada*" (so that one does not know) – we are able to free ourselves, at least temporarily, from the pseudo-knowledge and popular truisms that confuse us. We can shake off all of the accepted certainties that conceal the truth from us.

We are drunk with superficial illusions. We think that we have come this far, establishing a foothold in our homeland and embarking on the nascent beginnings of our national redemption, by virtue of our talents and wisdom. We forget that without the hand of the One "Who sows kindnesses and produces triumphs," all of our efforts would be for naught. We fail to perceive the Divine hand that is hidden behind all of our achievements.

---

1 Adapted from *Mo'adei HaRe'iyah*, pp. 266–267, from an article in *HaYesod* that Rav Kook penned on his last Purim in 1935.

All year long, we are drunk with a deceptive inebriation. We live unaware of the calculated plans of a greater world, a world ruled by the Master of the universe, with Whom we have a sworn pact guarding over Israel's eternal spirit. This covenant is ingrained in our very essence. It cannot be voided by evasion or alienation. Even if we should sink to the lowest level, we cannot change our skin, our body, our soul. Those who deceive themselves will suffer greatly until they return to where they are inherently connected. "His heart will understand, and he will return and will be healed" (Isaiah 6:10).

❧ A CALL TO UNITY

In the days of Mordechai and Esther, the Jewish people renewed their promise to keep the Torah (*Shabbat* 88a). In our days also, Esther's call to "Go, gather all of the Jews" should ring in our ears and stir the inner self to break forth from its place of hiding. The inner self, buried deeply in the soul of every Jew, resists the clever manipulations of misleading ideas and popular notions.

Let us reveal this epistle of Purim in all of its wonders, set above and beyond all of our superficial "knowledge." Let us announce the power of a united Israel, bringing together all sectors of the Jewish people. This is the secret strength of eternal Judaism. And through the strength of our unity we will be able to overcome all obstacles that stand in the way of our national rebirth.

מ

The Influence of Amalek[1]

THE TREACHEROUS ATTACK of Amalek, striking against the weak and helpless, was not a one-time enmity, an ancient grievance from our distant past. God commanded Moses to transmit the legacy of our struggle against Amalek for all generations:

> God instructed Moses, "Write this as a reminder in the book, and repeat it in Joshua's ears: I will utterly obliterate the memory of Amalek from under the heavens." ... God will be at war with Amalek for all generations.
>
> (Ex. 17:14,16)

✿ ERASABLE WRITING

The evil of Amalek invaded every aspect of our world. Even holy frameworks were not immune to this defiling influence. Therefore, they too require the possibility to be repaired by erasing, if necessary.

For this reason the Talmud (*Sotah* 17b)[2] rules that scribes should not add calcanthum (vitriol or sulfuric acid) to their ink, since calcanthum-enhanced ink cannot be erased by rubbing or washing. All writing – even

---

1   Adapted from *Igrot HaRe'iyah* vol. III, pp. 86–87 (1917).
2   See *Shulchan Aruch, Yoreh Dei'ah* 271:6; *Pitchei Teshuvah* ad loc 17.

holy books – must have the potential to be erased, as they may have been tainted by sparks of evil.

An extreme example of a holy object that has been totally contaminated is a Torah scroll written by a heretic. In such a case, it must be completely burned by fire.[3] Usually, however, holy objects only come in light contact with evil, and it is sufficient to ensure that the scribal ink is not permanent, so that the writing has the potential to be erased.

❧ THE UNIQUE TORAH OF RABBI MEIR

However, we find one scribe who did add calcanthum to his ink: the second-century scholar Rabbi Meir. Rabbi Meir was a unique individual. The Talmud states that there was none equal to Rabbi Meir in his generation. His teachings were so extraordinary that his colleagues were unable to fully follow his reasoning. Because of Rabbi Meir's exceptional brilliance, the Sages were hesitant to rule according to his opinion (*Eiruvin* 13a–b).

The Talmud further relates that Rabbi Meir's true name was not Meir. He was called Meir because "he would enlighten (*me'ir*) the eyes of the Sages in Halachah." What made Rabbi Meir's approach to Torah so unique? His teachings flowed from his aspiration to attain the future enlightenment of the Messianic Era. Because of this spiritual connection to the Messianic Era, the Jerusalem Talmud (*Kilayim* 9:3) conferred upon him the title "your messiah."

Rabbi Meir had no need to avoid using calcanthum, since his Torah belonged to the future era when Amalek's evil will be eradicated. On the contrary, he took care to enhance his ink, reflecting the eternal nature of his lofty teachings.

Rabbi Akiva, on the other hand, taught that scribes should not avail themselves of calcanthum. In the world's current state, everything must have the potential to be erased and corrected – even vessels of holy content. Only in this way will we succeed in totally obliterating Amalek and his malignant

---

3   *Gittin* 45b; *Shulchan Aruch, Yoreh Dei'ah* 281:1.

influence. Then we will halt the spread of evil traits in all peoples, the source of all private and public tragedy.

☙ UNITING THE ORAL AND WRITTEN LAW

The influence of Amalek had a second detrimental effect on the Torah. God commanded Moses to communicate the struggle against Amalek in two distinct channels. Moses transmitted God's message in writing – "Write this in the book" – and orally – "Repeat it in Joshua's ears." The refraction into divergent modes of transmission indicated that the Torah had lost some of its original unity.

Consequently, the Talmud in *Megillah* 18b rules that a scribe may not write from memory, not even a single letter. Our world maintains an entrenched division between the written and spoken word. Only with Amalek's obliteration and the world's redemption will we merit the unified light of the Torah's oral and written sides.

Once again, we find that Rabbi Meir and his Torah belonged to the future age, when this artificial split will no longer exist. Thus, when Rabbi Meir found himself in a place with no books, he wrote down the entire book of Esther from memory.

In the time of Mordechai and Esther, when we gained an additional measure of obliterating Amalek (with the defeat of Haman, a descendant of Amalek), the Torah regained some of its original unity. That generation accepted upon itself the Oral Law, in the same way that the Written Law had been accepted at Sinai (*Shabbat* 88a).

Timna and Purim[1]

The following description of Purim in Rav Kook's house during the years when he served as chief rabbi of Jaffa (1904–1914) was related by Rabbi Yeshaya Greenberg, headmaster of the Sha'arei Torah school in Jaffa:

THE JOY OVERFLOWED in the Rav's house during the Purim holiday. Breslov hassidim, who throughout the year were warmly received by Rav Kook, on Purim became the head merry-makers. Reb Meir Anshin and his friends would dance on the table, and the sounds of song and laughter drew many people to the Rav's house. Between songs and dances, Rav Kook spoke about the holiday, making frequent interruptions to drink a "*lechaim*." Any question or comment received an immediate rejoinder, with the Rav finding a direct connection to the holiday.

❧ REB MOSHE'S QUESTION

At one point, Reb Moshe Betzalel Todrosovich, a wealthy Jaffa merchant and philanthropist who was instrumental in bringing Rav Kook to Jaffa, entered the Rav's house. Reb Moshe had already finished his Purim meal

---

1   Adapted from *Mo'adei HaRe'iyah*, pp. 248–249.

at home, and being somewhat inebriated, requested that the Rav expound upon a verse that had no obvious connection to the holiday.

"Rebbe, please explain to us the verse, '*And the sister of Lotan was Timna*' (Gen. 36:22)."

Rav Kook raised his eyes, fixed his gaze on the questioner, and replied with a wide smile. "Why, Reb Moshe, that verse is integrally connected to Purim. In fact, the whole story of Purim begins from there!"

Reb Moshe was astounded. "Really? What does Lotan's sister have to do with Purim?"

❧ THE ROOT CAUSE OF AMALEK'S HATRED

Rav Kook then quoted the Talmudic statement in *Sanhedrin* 99b that Timna wanted to marry into the family of Abraham but was not accepted. In the end, she became the concubine of Esau's eldest son. "Better to be a maidservant to this people," Timna reasoned, "than a princess of another people." As punishment for rejecting Timna, the Jewish people were cursed with the eternal enmity of Timna's son – Amalek.

This of course is the connection to the story of Purim, for Haman, the enemy of the Jews, was a descendant of Amalek. Haman's hatred of the Jews and his decree to destroy them in fact originated in the failure to convert his great-grandmother Timna. But this error was redressed in the time of Mordechai and Esther, when "Many of the peoples of the land became Jews" (Esther 8:17).

Rav Kook continued to expound on this topic for two hours, drawing from both Halachic and Aggadic sources, quoting the Zohar and Maimonides, his words shining with brilliance and erudition. When he finally concluded, Reb Moshe jumped up, grabbed the Rav and hugged him, crying, "Rebbe, I love you!"

PASSOVER פסח

The Ongoing Process of Redemption

The redemption continues onward. The redemption from Egypt and the final redemption of the future is one uninterrupted act. The process of the "strong hand and the outstretched arm"[1] that began in Egypt continues its influence in all subsequent events.

Moses and Elijah work to bring the same redemption.[2] One begins and one concludes; together they complete a single unit.

(Orot, p. 44)

---

1   Deut. 4:35. The word "hand" in Hebrew (ידו, מיד, עלידו) has the connotation of near and immediate, within one's grasp. "Arm," on the other hand, indicates that one is reaching out for something distant. [The word for "arm" (זרוע) comes from the root-word זרע (seed), implying a future outcome.] Thus the phrase "strong hand" indicates the actual and the immediate – God's intervention in Egypt – while "outstretched arm" indicates the potential and the future, i.e., the ongoing process of redemption throughout the ages until the final redemption. See "The Strong Hand and the Outstretched Arm," below.
2   Moses was God's emissary for the redemption in Egypt, while Elijah will be the harbinger of the final redemption.

Who is Free?[1]

THE MAJOR THEME of the Passover holiday is, undoubtedly, freedom. But we must understand what this freedom is all about. Does it refer simply to the end of Egyptian slavery? Is it only political independence – a gift which has eluded the Jewish people for most of their 4,000-year existence?

‌ TRUE TO OUR INNER ESSENCE

The difference between a slave and a free person is not merely a matter of social position. We may find an enlightened slave whose spirit is free, and a free man with the mindset of a slave.

True freedom is that proud and indomitable spirit by which the individual – as well as the nation as a whole – is determined to remain faithful to his inner essence, to the spiritual dimension of the Divine image within. It is this quality that gives meaning and purpose to life.

Individuals with a slave mentality live their lives and expresses views that are based, not on their own essential spiritual nature, but on that which is attractive and good in the eyes of others. In this way they are ruled by others, whether physically or by social convention, in body or in spirit.

---

1   Adapted from *Ma'amarei HaRe'iyah*, pp. 157–158.

Vanquished and exiled, the Jewish people were oppressed over the centuries by cruel masters. But our inner soul always remained imbued with the spirit of freedom. Were it not for the wondrous gift of the Torah, bestowed upon us when we left Egypt for eternal freedom, the long and bitter exile would have crushed our spirits and reduced us to a slave mentality. But on Passover, the festival of freedom, we openly demonstrate that we are free in our very essence, and our yearnings for that which is good and holy are a genuine reflection of our inner nature.

Aiming for Greatness[1]

WE ARE CHARGED to sing out in joy – God answered our prayers and rescued us from the bondage of Egyptian slavery:

אָנֹכִי ה' אֱלֹהֶיךָ הַמַּעַלְךָ מֵאֶרֶץ מִצְרָיִם. הַרְחֶב־פִּיךָ וַאֲמַלְאֵהוּ. (תהילים פא:יא)

I am the Eternal your God Who raises you up from the land of Egypt. Open your mouth wide and I will fill it. (Psalm 81:11)

What is the connection between our redemption from Egypt and "opening our mouths wide" to receive God's blessings?

❧ ONGOING ELEVATION

A careful reading of this verse will note two peculiarities about the word *ha-maalcha*, "Who raises you up." First of all, it does not say that God "took you out" of Egypt, but that He "raises you up." It was not merely the act of leaving Egypt that made its eternal impact on the destiny of the Jewish nation, and through it, all of humanity. The Exodus was an act of elevation, lifting up the souls of Israel.

Additionally, the verse is not in the past tense but in the present – "Who *raises* you up." Is it not referring to a historical event? We may understand

1   Adapted from *Olat Re'iyah* vol. I, pp. 219–220.

this in light of the Midrash (*Tanchuma Mikeitz* 10) concerning the creation of the universe. The Midrash states that when God commanded the formation of the *rakiya*, the expanse between the upper and lower waters (Gen. 1:6), the divide between the heavens and the earth began to expand. This expansion would have continued indefinitely had the Creator not halted it by commanding, "Enough!"[2] In other words, unless they are meant only for a specific hour, Divine acts are eternal, continuing forever. So too, the spiritual ascent of "raising you up from Egypt" is a perpetual act of God, influencing and uplifting the Jewish people throughout the generations.

There is no limit to this elevation, no end to our spiritual aspirations. The only limitations come from us, if we choose to restrict our wishes and dreams. But once we know the secret of *ha-ma'alcha* and internalize the message of a Divine process that began in Egypt and continues to elevate us, we can aim for ever-higher spiritual goals.

It is instructive to note the contrast between the Hebrew word for "Egypt" – *Mitzrayim*, literally, "limitations" – and the expression, "open up wide." God continually frees us from the confining restraints of *Mitzrayim*, enabling us to strive for the highest, most expansive aspirations.

Now we may understand why the verse concludes with the charge, "Open your mouth wide." We should not restrict ourselves. We need to rise above all self-imposed limitations and transcend all mundane goals and petty objectives. If we can "open our mouths wide" and recognize our true potential for spiritual greatness, then "I will fill it" – God will help us attain ever-higher levels of holiness.

---

2 The Midrash thus explains the Name *Sha-dai* ("Almighty") as echoing the Divine cry of "*Dai*" ("Enough") to the universe, preventing it from expanding indefinitely.

Destroy Chametz, Gain Freedom[1]

BY THE FIRST day [of Passover] you must clear out your homes of all
leaven.   (Ex. 12:15)

✦ WHY CLEAR OUT *CHAMETZ*?

Why does the Torah command us to destroy all *chametz* (leaven) found
in our homes during Passover? It is logical to eat matzah; this fast-baked
food has a historical connection to the Exodus, recalling our hurried escape
from Egyptian slavery. But how does clearing out leaven from our homes
relate to the Passover theme of freedom and independence?

✦ FREEDOM OF SPIRIT

There are two aspects to attaining true freedom. First, one needs to be
physically independent of all foreign subjugation. But complete freedom
also requires freedom of the spirit. The soul is not free if it is subjected to
external demands that prevent it from following the path of its inner truth.

The difference between a slave and a free person is not just a matter of
social standing. One may find an educated slave whose spirit is free, and a

---

1   Adapted from *Olat Re'iyah* vol. II, p. 244.

free person with the mindset of a slave. What makes us truly free? When we are able to be faithful to our inner self, to the truth of our Divine image – then we can live a fulfilled life, a life focused on our soul's inner goals. One whose spirit is servile, on the other hand, will never experience this sense of self-fulfillment. His happiness will always depend upon the approval of others who dominate over him, whether this control is *de jure* or *de facto*.

❧ THE FOREIGN INFLUENCE OF LEAVEN

What is *chametz*? Leaven is a foreign substance added to the dough. The leavening agent makes the dough rise; it changes its natural shape and characteristics. Destruction of all leaven in the house symbolizes the removal of all foreign influences and constraints that prevent us from realizing our spiritual aspirations.

These two levels of independence, physical and spiritual, exist on both the individual and the national level. An independent people must be free not only from external rule, but also from foreign domination in the cultural and spiritual spheres.

For the Israelites in Egypt, it was precisely at the hour of imminent redemption that the dangers of these foreign "leavening" forces were the greatest. At that time of great upheaval, true permanent emancipation was not a given. Would the Israelites succeed in freeing themselves, not only from Egyptian bondage, but also from the idolatrous culture in which they had lived for hundreds of years? To commemorate their complete liberation from Egypt, the Passover holiday of freedom requires the removal of all foreign "leavening" agents.

❧ CLEANSING OURSELVES OF FOREIGN INFLUENCES

In our days too, an analogous era of imminent redemption, we need to purge the impure influences of alien cultures and attitudes that have entered our national spirit during our long exile among the nations.

Freedom is the fulfillment of our inner essence. We need to aspire to the lofty freedom of those who left Egypt. To the Israelites of that generation, God revealed Himself and brought them into His service. This is truly the highest form of freedom, as the Sages taught in *Avot* (6:2):

> Instead of "engraved (*charut*) on the tablets" (Ex. 32:16), read it as "freedom" (*cheirut*). Only one who studies Torah is truly free.

The Strong Hand and the Outstretched Arm[1]

REMEMBER ... the strong hand and the outstretched arm with which the Eternal your God brought you out [of Egypt]. (Deut. 7:18–19)

We are familiar with the phrase הַיָּד הַחֲזָקָה וְהַזְּרֹעַ הַנְּטוּיָה from the Haggadah, read every year on Passover. But what exactly do the "strong hand" and "outstretched arm" refer to?

✎ STRONG HAND – DRAMATIC TRANSFORMATION

If the objective of the Exodus had been only to liberate the Israelites and raise them to the level of other free nations of the world, then no special Divine intervention would have been necessary. By the usual laws of nature and history, the Jewish people would have gradually progressed to a level of culture and morality prevalent among nations.

However, God wanted the newly freed slaves to swiftly attain a high moral and spiritual plane. In order to prepare them for their unique destiny, they required God's "strong hand." This metaphor implies a forceful intervention that neutralized the natural forces of the universe. God's "strong

---

1   Adapted from *Olat Re'iyah* vol. II, pp. 279–283.

hand" dramatically raised the Jewish people from the depths of defilement and degradation in Egypt to the spiritual heights of Sinai.

We commemorate this sudden elevation of the people, the "strong hand," by eating the rapidly-baked matzah. This rationale for eating matzah is stated explicitly in the Haggadah: "Because there was not time for the dough of our fathers to leaven before the King of all kings, the Holy One, revealed Himself to them and redeemed them."

ꝏ OUTSTRETCHED ARM – TOWARD THE FUTURE

The "outstretched arm," on the other hand, implies an unrealized potential, a work in progress. The Hebrew word for "arm" is *zero'a*, from the root *zera* (seed), indicating future growth. Even today, the ultimate goal of the Exodus has still not been fully achieved. The process of perfecting and redeeming the Jewish people is one of gradual progression.

If matzah commemorates the sudden redemptive quality of God's "strong hand," which Passover mitzvah symbolizes the "outstretched arm"? That would be the *maror*, the bitter herbs. The *maror* reminds us of the bitterness of slavery. The very fact that we felt this bitterness is an indication that servitude contradicts our true essence. By virtue of our inner nature, we will slowly but surely realize our true potential.

While the "strong hand" gave the initial push, it is through the "outstretched arm" that we steadily advance toward our final goal. This gradual progress is accomplished through the mitzvot, which refine and elevate us. It is for this reason that all mitzvot are fundamentally connected to the redemption from Egypt.

꩜

"Because of This"[1]

AFTER COMMANDING US to commemorate the date we left Egypt, the Torah also instructs us to transmit these memories to the next generation.

וְהִגַּדְתָּ לְבִנְךָ בַּיּוֹם הַהוּא לֵאמֹר: בַּעֲבוּר זֶה עָשָׂה ה' לִי בְּצֵאתִי מִמִּצְרָיִם. (שמות יג:ח)

On that day you must tell your child, "It is because of this that God acted for me when I left Egypt." (Ex. 13:8)

The wording, however, is unclear. "Because of this" – what does the word "this" refer to? What is the reason that, for its sake, God performed the signs and miracles in Egypt?

֍ MEMORIES FOR ALL GENERATIONS

One might think that the sole function of the ten plagues was to rescue the Israelites from persecution and slavery. In fact, the true goal of the miracles in Egypt goes far beyond the needs of that generation. Those historic events were meant to create an eternal inheritance for all generations. Their purpose is achieved as each generation preserves these national memories and transmits them to the next generation.

---

1   Adapted from *Olat Re'iyah* vol. I, p. 39.

This is how the verse should be understood. The word "this" refers back to the beginning of the verse. "It is because of this" – so that "you will tell your child" – "that God acted for me when I left Egypt." The ultimate purpose of the signs and wonders in Egypt is fulfilled as each generation absorbs the elevated impressions of those miracles, drawing from them their great light and holiness.

According to the Haggadah's exegesis, "because of this" refers to the special foods that we eat to recall the Exodus: "The Passover Seder may not be conducted until the time when matzah and bitter herbs are set before you." This does not contradict the explanation presented above; it simply adds an additional nuance. We commemorate the Exodus and recount its story to the next generation when we can physically point to the matzah and bitter herbs on Passover night. According to this explanation, the purpose of the Exodus is accomplished when we experientially transmit to our children the smells, tastes, and memories of that historic event.

Answering the Wise Child[1]

THE HAGGADAH SPEAKS of four children. Each one asks his own question, and each one receives a personal response. Education, the Sages taught, is not something that can be mass-produced like a Model-T.

The first child, the wise son, is troubled by the Torah's abundance of rituals and minutiae. For the intelligent and rational, everything should be logical. What meaning can there be in these myriad details and rules? "What is the meaning of the rituals, rules, and laws that the Eternal our God has commanded you?" (Deut. 6:20)

✦ WHY ALL THE DETAILS?

In one brief query, the wise child has challenged the very foundations of a religion rich in customs and traditions. Why do we need all of these details and *halachot*? Why is it not enough to abide by Judaism's basic tenets and fundamental teachings?

The Haggadah's response is enigmatic, ostensibly irrelevant to the question:

---

1   Adapted from *Olat Re'iyah* vol. II, p. 275.

You shall explain to him the laws of Passover: one does not eat any dessert after the paschal offering.

Are we to explain to him all the laws of Passover? Or just this one rule about not eating after the paschal offering – or nowadays, the *afikoman-matzah* – has been eaten at the end of the meal? What is the significance of this particular rule?

⋅⋅ THE SEDER FROG

I recall one year my six-year-old daughter was bursting with excitement, watching us unpack the Passover dishes. The special pots and pans that she fondly remembered from last Passover were back once again!

Then we uncovered a small piece of green velvet-cloth that fits over a finger. Once upon a time it sported two plastic eyes and even a little red tongue. Our eldest brought it home from kindergarten one year, and ever since it has graced our Seder table, making a special appearance during the passage about the plague of frogs.

This year, I wondered: would my daughter recognize this lump of green cloth, only on display for a few minutes each year? But I need not have worried. Her face immediately lit up as she spied the Passover Seder "frog."

⋅⋅ ETCHING THE MITZVAH ON OUR SOUL

The detailed laws of mitzvot serve a crucial function. They create an atmosphere and enhance the mitzvah-experience. They deepen the impression the mitzvah makes on the soul. Our intense involvement in all aspects of mitzvot leads to a deeper love of God, the ultimate Source for the Torah's mitzvot.

Thus, for the wise and logical child, we specifically mention the rule about not eating after the *afikoman*. Why is matzah the very last food we eat on Seder night? We want the experience of Passover to make a deep and lasting impression. We want the taste of matzah to remain in our mouths for as long as possible. So we eat the *afikoman* at the very end of the meal, even after dessert.

The detailed laws surrounding each mitzvah etch the experience of that mitzvah onto our souls. Like the matzah on Passover, we want the taste of the mitzvah to stay with us as long as possible. Just as our own personal additions to Passover customs – even formless pieces of faded green velvet – will conjure up images of frolicking frogs and past Passovers, evoking childhood memories of celebration and thanksgiving engraved deeply on the soul.

Priceless Jewels on Tattered Clothes[1]

Every year at the Passover Seder we read Ezekiel's allegorical description of the Jewish people in Egypt:

> You grew big and tall; you came with great adornments and were beautiful of form, with flowing hair. But you were naked and bare. (Ezekiel 16:7)

The prophet describes the Israelites as being large and numerous, yet, at the same time, impoverished and barren. Physically, Jacob's family of seventy souls had developed into a large nation. Despite Egyptian persecution and oppression, they had become numerous. Morally and spiritually, however, they were "naked and bare."

What about the "great adornments" that the verse mentions? What were these "jewels" of Israel?

TWO SPECIAL JEWELS

These "jewels" symbolize two special traits of the Jewish people. The first trait is a natural propensity for spirituality, an inner desire never to be separated from God and holiness.

The second "jewel" is an even greater gift, beyond the natural realm. It is

1 Adapted from *Olat Re'iyah* vol. II, p. 276.

the unique communal spirit of Israel that aspires to a lofty national destiny. Even in their dispirited state as downtrodden slaves in Egypt, their inner drive for national purpose burned like a glowing coal. It smoldered in the heart of each individual, even if many did not understand its true nature.

For the Hebrew slaves, however, these special qualities were like priceless diamonds pinned on the threadbare rags of an unkempt beggar. The people lacked the basic traits of decency and integrity. They were missing those ethical qualities that are close to human nature, like clothes that are worn next to the body.

Without a fundamental level of morality and proper conduct, their unique yearnings for spiritual greatness had the sardonic effect of extravagant jewelry pinned to tattered clothes. "You came with great adornments . . . but you were naked and bare."

The Special Pesach Offering[1]

THE OFFERING BROUGHT for the Passover holiday, the *korban pesach*, has special laws how it is to be cooked and eaten:

> They will eat the meat on that night ... Do not eat it raw, or cooked in water, but only roasted over fire. (Ex. 12:8–9)

Why may the *korban pesach* only be eaten at the nighttime? And why must it be roasted?

৯৹ NATIONAL HOLINESS IN EACH INDIVIDUAL

All Temple offerings fall into two categories. Some are *korbanot yachid*, personal offerings brought by the individual; while others are *korbanot tzibur*, communal offerings brought in the name of the entire nation. An individual brings a *korban yachid* for private reasons – to atone for a particular sin or express gratitude for a personal deliverance. The Jewish nation as a whole, on the other hand, is represented by communal offerings which commemorate national events and holidays.

Of all the Temple offerings, the *korban pesach* is unique, since it combines characteristics of both categories of offerings. It commemorates a national

---

1 Adapted from *Olat Re'iyah* vol. I, pp. 178–179.

historic event; and yet the obligation to bring this offering is not on the nation but on the individual. Why is it not like other communal offerings?

This unusual offering teaches us an important lesson about the Jewish people. The *korban pesach* reveals the quality of national holiness that resides in the soul of every Jew. Our ties to *Knesset Yisrael* are so deep that each individual's *pesach* offering is like a *korban tzibur* representing the entire nation. And the special connection of each individual to the nation is reflected in the laws regulating how the *korban pesach* is to be eaten.

❧ THE UNITY OF ISRAEL

Our daytime activities are characterized by extensive social interaction, while at night we retire to our homes and private lives. By stipulating that the Passover offering be eaten at night, the Torah is emphasizing that our connection to the Jewish people is not based on some form of social contract, a utilitarian agreement to band together due to common interests. Rather, our ties to the Jewish people reflect a unique shared commonality that binds together all of Israel. These national ties persist *even at night*, a time when each individual retreats to the privacy of his home.

The manner in which the offering is cooked is similarly instructive. Were it boiled in water or cooked together with other foods, the taste of the *korban* would spread outside of the meat. Roasting, on the other hand, prevents the flavor from dispersing to other foods. This ensures that the offering's qualities of holiness remain concentrated inside the *korban pesach*. Why should this experience be so intense?

The mitzvah of eating the roasted offering has the power to uplift each individual with an intensity of pure holiness, a powerful quality rooted in the national soul of Israel. This concentrated holiness deepens our awareness of the singular unity of Israel, a result of the communal holiness that resides within each and every individual, in all of his being.

The "Hillel Sandwich"[1]

TOGETHER OR SEPARATE? The Sages disagreed on how one should
eat the matzah and maror (bitter herbs) at the Passover Seder.

The Talmud in *Berachot* 49a admonishes us not to perform
mitzvot "bundled together" ("*chavilot chavilot*"). We do not want to give
the impression that mitzvot are an unwanted burden, an obligation that we
wish to discharge as quickly as possible. For this reason, the majority opinion
is that the two mitzvot of eating matzah and maror should be performed
separately.

But Hillel's custom was to place the *pesach* offering and the maror inside
the matzah and eat them together like a sandwich. Why did Hillel combine
these mitzvot together?

॰ MATZAH AND FREEDOM

To understand Hillel's opinion we must first examine the significance of
matzah and maror. Matzah is a symbol of freedom. But what *is* freedom?
Freedom does not mean sitting idle and unoccupied. True freedom means
the opportunity to grow and develop according to one's inner nature and
natural gifts, without interference or coercion from outside influences. This

---

1   Adapted from *Olat Re'iyah* vol. II, pp. 287–289.

freedom is symbolized by matzah, a simple food consisting solely of flour and water, unaffected by other ingredients and chemical processes.

In order to form the Jewish people as a holy nation, their national character needed to be independent of all foreign influences. They left Egypt free from the spiritual baggage of Egyptian culture. Thus we find that in preparation of bringing the Passover offering, they were commanded to "draw out and take for yourselves sheep" (Ex. 12:21). What does it mean to "draw out"? The Midrash explains that they needed to remove from within themselves any affinity to Egyptian idolatry (*Mechilta* ad loc).

With a clean slate, lacking any national character of their own, a holy character could then be imprinted on Israel's national soul. This is part of the metaphor of matzah: it lacks any shape and taste of its own, so that the desired form and flavor may be properly imposed upon it.

❧ THE MESSAGE OF MAROR

Maror is the opposite of matzah; its bitterness is a symbol of servitude. But even servitude may have a positive value. An individual whose life's ambition is to become a doctor must spend many years in medical school to achieve this goal. The long years of concentrated effort require great dedication and discipline. These years are a form of servitude – but a servitude that advances one's final goal, and thus is ultimately a true expression of freedom.

This idea may also be applied to the Jewish people. Our souls are ingrained with a Divine nature, but we suffer from character imperfections that prevent us from realizing our inner nature. For this reason we need to accept upon ourselves a pleasant form of servitude, the service of God. We acquired this ability in Egypt. This is slavery's positive contribution – it teaches one to accept the deferment of immediate desires and short-term goals.

This is the central message of maror: acceptance of life's bitter aspects, with the knowledge that this forbearance and resolve will allow us to attain higher objectives. For this reason, we eat the maror only *after* eating the matzah – only after we have clarified our ultimate goals.

DISCIPLINE AND FREEDOM

Now we may better understand the disagreement between Hillel and the other sages. Freedom, as symbolized by the matzah, reveals the inherent holiness of Israel and our natural love for God and Torah. This innate character enables us to overcome desires that do not concur with our elevated goals. It is through our persistence and dedication to the overall goal that we reveal our inner resources of freedom.

Both of these traits, freedom and servitude, need to be free to act without interference from one another. When a spirit of freedom and independence is appropriate, it should not be constrained by a servile attitude; and when discipline and a sense of duty are needed, they should not be disrupted by a desire for freedom. Thus, according to the majority opinion, we should eat the matzah and maror separately, indicating that each trait should be expressed to its fullest.

The ultimate goal, however, is attained only when we recognize that these two forces do not contradict one another. Joined together, they present the highest freedom, whose nobility and power is fully revealed when it wears the crown of lofty servitude – the service of the Holy King, a service that is freedom in its purest state.

Thus Hillel would eat the matzah and maror together. He sought to emphasize that freedom and slavery are not contradictory concepts. Generally speaking, the quality of servitude belongs more to the preparatory stage; but in the overall picture, the two forces are interrelated, complementing one another to attain the final goal.

Shir HaShirim – The Song of Songs[1]

❧ THE SEASHORE ESSAY

It was 1901, at a summer resort on the Baltic Sea. A young graduate of the Telshe yeshiva, troubled by matters of faith, opened his heart and his questions to the erudite young rabbi of Boisk – Rav Kook – who was vacationing there.

During an excursion to the seashore, their conversation turned to the book of *Shir HaShirim*, the Song of Songs. Rav Kook gave a brilliant exposition on the nature of this poem of love, and in general, the place of romance and love in literature. The novel ideas vividly stirred the young man. In fact, he entreated Rav Kook to stop. He knew the conversation would continue to other topics, and he feared losing this rare gem. He hurried to retrieve a pen and paper so that the rabbi could write down the ideas he had just expounded on. Rav Kook acceded to his request, and so, after his return with writing implements, the Rav spent the next few minutes perched on a rock by the roaring sea, writing down his thoughts on *Shir HaShirim*.

---

1   Adapted from *Olat Re'iyah*, vol. II, pp. 3–4. Historical notes from *Mo'adei HaRe'iyah*, pp. 333–334. (I have included this article here in accordance with the custom to read *Shir HaShirim* on the Sabbath that falls during the intermediate days of Passover.)

Not long after this incident, the editor of the journal *Mizrach* suggested that Rav Kook submit an article to be included in the next issue. The young man excitedly proposed sending the short essay written on the seashore, and Rav Kook agreed. The essay subsequently made its way into a number of other periodicals, until it was eventually printed in *Olat Re'iyah*, Rav Kook's commentary on the prayer book.

The young man later became well-known as a prominent scholar – Rabbi Dr. Benjamin Menashe Lewin, author of the monumental work *Otzar HaGaonim*.

THE ROLE OF ART

What is the purpose of Literature, and Art in general?

The purpose of Art, in all its forms, is to give expression to every concept, every emotion, and every thought found in the depths of the human soul. As long as even one quality remains concealed within the soul, it is the responsibility of the artist to reveal it.

Of course, artistic expression is not without boundaries and limits. The artist is duty-bound to create and express as long as his art serves to enrich and ennoble life. Some matters, however, are best left hidden. For such topics, the artist should use his figurative shovel, to bury and cover (cf. Deut. 23:24). Woe to the author who uses his artistic tools for the opposite purpose, to uncover and reveal unseemly matters, thus polluting the general atmosphere.

LOVE AND LITERATURE

What about romance and love? How should literature relate to these delicate topics?

The intense emotions that are experienced with regard to love are a significant part of the human condition, and it is natural that literature should expound on them. Great care, however, is required when dealing with this particular subject. The tendency toward intoxication with these emotions can defile the subject's inherent purity.

It is unfortunate that modern literature concerns itself exclusively with only one form of love – the romantic love between man and woman. If a literary work without some expression of the inner feelings of romantic love is considered incomplete, then it certainly should include some of man's lofty emotions of love for the Creator of all works, the Source of all good and kindness. Can the depths of this exquisite love be measured? Can it be contained within vast oceans or confined within expansive skies?

The dearth of artistic expression for this sublime love is redressed by the Bible's lofty song of love: the Song of Songs. As Rabbi Akiva taught: "All the books of the Bible are holy; but the Song of Songs is the Holy of Holies" (*Yadayim* 3:5).

ℑ⊛ RABBI AKIVA AND *SHIR HASHIRIM*

A soul that is insensitive to feelings of romance cannot relate to the tender sensibilities expressed in songs of love. Such a person will pervert those poetic yearnings, reducing them to the level of his own base desires. Similarly, one who has never ascended the heights of holy contemplation, one who has never experienced the uplifting surge of love for the Rock of all worlds – such a person will fail to grasp how the sublime yearnings of the Song of Songs truly reflect the highest aspirations of the Jewish people. But an insightful person will recognize that the body of literature of this holy nation, whose long history is replete with extraordinary displays of self-sacrifice and martyrdom to sanctify God's Name, would be incomplete without a suitable expression of their boundless love for God.

As he was cruelly put to death at the hands of the Romans, Rabbi Akiva told his students, "All my life I have been troubled by this verse, 'You will love God ... with all your soul' – even if he takes your soul. When will I have the opportunity to fulfill this?" Rabbi Akiva then recited the *Shema*, and his soul departed when he reached the word *echad*, declaring God's unity (*Berachot* 61b).

Only a soul as great as Rabbi Akiva could testify that the Song of Songs is the Holy of Holies, and that "the entire universe is unworthy of the day that the Song of Songs was given to Israel." In his life, Rabbi Akiva experienced love in all of its levels: the private love for Kalba Savua's daughter, in its natural purity; the idealistic love for his people, including its fight for independence against Roman occupation; and the lofty love for God, in all of its noble beauty. Thus Rabbi Akiva was eminently qualified to evaluate the true nature of the love so poetically expressed in the Song of Songs.

But those with narrow minds and coarse hearts cannot properly appreciate this precious book. They are like those who crawl at the bottom of a towering castle that stretches high into the clouds. They measure the height of this great edifice according to their limited eyesight. And if they are informed that from the spires of this great castle one may view a dazzling star, breathtaking in its exquisite beauty, they immediately conclude that such a star must be a lowly one indeed.

Such narrow minds, who can only see in Rabbi Akiva a lonely shepherd who fell in love with his employer's daughter, will certainly fail to comprehend his startling declaration that the Song of Songs is sacred above all other books of the Bible. They only see a simple shepherd and a simple song of private love.

We may appreciate Rabbi Akiva's greatness of soul from the following story. When a group of scholars saw a fox scampering in the ruins where the holy Temple once stood, they shed tears at this sight of bleak desolation. Rabbi Akiva, however, astounded his companions by laughing. He understood that, just as the prophecies of destruction had come to pass, the prophecies of redemption will also be fulfilled. For this spiritual giant, the distant future was as real and palpable as the present reality. His unshakable faith and vision was rooted in a profound love of God. This love so filled his pure heart that the future was a certain reality, leaving no room to mourn over the disasters of the present. For Rabbi Akiva, the tragedies of the day were but a thin cloud, casting fleeting shadows under the brilliant daytime sun.

Only such a lofty soul could confidently proclaim, "The entire Bible is holy. But the Song of Songs is the Holy of Holies."

ISRAEL INDEPENDENCE DAY

יום העצמאות

A Divine Movement

The great vision of our national rebirth is not the product of the deliberations of the human heart or the spirit of mortal man. This vision is the word of God. A ray of holy light of the God of Israel is revealed in all of our movements, great and small.

The national movement dedicated to building the nation in the land of Israel is an openly Divine movement, created by the Holy One of Israel. It is destined to restore honor and dignity to God's people, and renew their enlightening influence on the world and life in general.

(Igrot HaRe'iyah vol. III, p. 216; Mo'adei HaRe'iyah, p. 391)

Rav Kook and Zionism[1]

URING CONTROVERSY OVER the *Hetter Mechirah*[2] in 1910, Rabbi Yaakov David Wilovsky (the "Ridbaz") of Safed leveled a serious accusation. He accused Rav Kook of abandoning his religious beliefs and becoming a Zionist in his old age. (In fact, from a very early age Rav Kook was imbued with a great love for *Eretz Yisrael*.)

For an Orthodox rabbi to support a secular movement that publicly proclaimed that it "has nothing to do with theology"[3] was close to heresy. Why should a religious scholar with a deep love for all peoples be supportive of a secular nationalist movement? Indeed, Rav Kook's outlook on Zionism is a complex topic, the subject of numerous books and academic articles, and certainly beyond the scope of a brief essay. Nonetheless, the following excerpts from his writings and letters shed light on his views on this non-religious (and sometimes anti-religious) movement.

---

1. Based on letters from *Igrot HaRe'iyah* vol. I, pp. 56, 88, 207–208 (1907); vol. I, p. 448 (1910); vol. II, pp. 171–172, 194–195 (1913); vol. III, pp. 157–158 (1918).
2. A legal fiction of selling the land in order to circumvent the prohibition of working the land during the Sabbatical year.
3. So announced Max Nordau, vice-president of the Zionist movement, in 1897. (Herzl, however, disassociated himself from this pronouncement.)

❧ HISTORICAL PRECEDENTS

Rav Kook noted that our generation is not the first to experience a return to the land of Israel comprised primarily of Jews lax in religious observance. When Ezra led the return to *Eretz Yisrael* in the beginning of the Second Temple Period, many of the Jewish pioneers who joined him were Sabbath-desecrators and worse; and yet this period witnessed the rebuilding of the Temple and tremendous advances in Torah scholarship.

Centuries later, during the corrupt reign of Herod, the nation suffered from a cruel king, far removed from the ideal Jewish leader. The irony of the holy Temple built by Herod, a brutal and paranoid despot, is even greater than the current phenomenon of the Holy Land being resettled by secular pioneers. The actual construction, Rav Kook wrote, "may be carried by those who fail to penetrate the profound secrets of the righteous. And not just the stonemasons; they may even be the ones orchestrating the construction." Yet this does not sully the innate purity of the lofty objective.

❧ THE POSITIVE INFLUENCE OF *ERETZ YISRAEL*

Rav Kook suggested that we need not be overly concerned about the religious level of the pioneers, since the Land on its own will determine who is deserving of living in it.

> There is no need to check the level of *kashrut* of those who come, for the Land will vomit out the true chaff; and "all those remaining shall be called holy" (Isaiah 4:3). This is similar to how we do not separate food from its waste elements before we eat it, but leave this [separation] process to life's natural functions.

Furthermore, the merit of *Eretz Yisrael* helps even the unworthy:

> The merit of the Land even protects the wicked. Even a gentile maidservant in the land of Israel is promised a portion in the World to Come (*Ketubot* 111a). Clearly the Talmud is not speaking of a righteous maidservant, who

would anyway merit the World to Come ... Rather it is referring to an ordinary maidservant, with sordid deeds and coarse traits. Nonetheless, the merit of living in the land of Israel enables her to gain a portion in the World to Come. ...

All the more so [regarding the secular Zionists, since] one may find in every Jew, even the most unworthy, precious gems of good deeds and positive traits. Certainly the land of Israel helps elevate and sanctify them. And if this is not evident in them, it will become so in their descendants.

❧ SACRED ROOTS

Despite the current secular nature of Zionism, the return to *Eretz Yisrael* in recent times was first promoted by great *tzaddikim* – starting with the disciples of the Gaon of Vilna and the Baal Shem Tov – and Zionism derives its spiritual nourishment from these holy roots.

> [It was] the lofty righteous of previous generations who ignited a holy inner fire, a burning love for the holiness of *Eretz Yisrael* in the hearts of God's people. Due to their efforts, individuals gathered in the desolate land, until significant areas became a garden of Eden, and a large and important community of the entire people of Israel has settled in our holy land. ...
>
> Recently, however, the pious and great scholars have gradually abandoned the enterprise of settling the Holy Land. ... This holy work has been appropriated by those lacking in [Torah] knowledge and good deeds. ... Nonetheless, we see that the [secularists'] dedication in deed and action is nourished from the initial efforts of true *tzaddikim*, who kindled the holy desire to rebuild the Holy Land and return our exiles there.

❧ BREAKING OF THE VESSELS

For Rav Kook, the fall of Zionism into the hands of the secularists was a form of *shevirat keilim*, reminiscent of the Kabbalistic "breaking of vessels" that occurred when the universe was created. The original light and holiness was simply too great to be contained within the limitations of the physical vessels; and it is our task to return these fallen sparks to their elevated source.[4]

But why did the return to the land of Israel need to be appropriated by a secular nationalist movement? Rav Kook attempted to solve this riddle by noting certain qualities lacking in religious circles:

> The fundamental moral force hidden in [the Zionist movement] ... is its motto, "the entire nation." This nationalism proclaims ... that it seeks to redeem the entire Jewish people. It does not concern itself with individuals or parties or sectors. ... And with this perspective, it reaches out to the land of Israel and the love of Zion with a remarkable bravery and courage.
>
> It is clear that we cannot confront this adversary if we lack the same noble sense of responsibility that speaks in the name of the entire nation, all of Israel. We may not distinguish and divide. We may not say, "This one is one of ours so we will take care of him, but not that one." ... [We must] care in our hearts and souls for the good of the entire nation and its redemption, in the most inclusive way possible.

Additionally, Rav Kook explained that the pre-Messianic era requires a more practical, down-to-earth orientation, so that the Jewish people may return to their land as a healthy, balanced nation, after centuries of detached statelessness in exile.

> We have a tradition[5] that there will be a spiritual revolt of the Jewish people in *Eretz Yisrael* during the initial period of national revival. ... The aspirations for lofty and holy ideals will cease and the nation's spirit will sink. ... The necessity for this revolt will be the tendency for materialism,

---

4   When questioned once about the phenomenon of secularists resettling the Land, Rav Kook responded by quoting the Talmudic explanation how repairs and renovations are carried out in the Temple: "[The workmen] build in non-holy state, and afterward it is sanctified" (*Me'ilah* 14a).

5   "In the footsteps of the Messiah, arrogance will increase and respect will dwindle .... The government will turn to heresy and none will offer rebuke .... The wisdom of scholars will deteriorate, the pious will be despised, and the truth will be nowhere to be found. Youths will disgrace their elders; the elderly will stand in the presence of youth" (*Sotah* 49b).

which must be powerfully generated in the entire nation after the passage
of so many years in which the need and availability of material pursuits
were completely absent. When born, this proclivity will trample angrily
and stir up storms; these are the birth pangs of the Messianic era.

(*Orot HaTechiyah* sec. 44, p. 84)

However, secular Zionism can only bring about the material rebuilding
of the Jewish people in their homeland. The nation's complete renewal will
only come about when Zionism is restored to its original holiness.

Secular nationalism may be defiled with much defilement, concealing
many evil spirits. But we will not succeed by trying to expel this movement from the nation's soul. Rather we must energetically return it to its
elevated source and combine it with the original holiness from which it
emanates. (*Orot HaTechiyah* sec. 22, p. 75)

ஃ TRUE ZIONISM

And what about the Ridbaz's accusations that Rav Kook had descended
to heresy, becoming a secular Zionist? Rav Kook responded that Zionism,
when based on its true ideals, is nothing to be ashamed of:

My dear friend! If all Zionists would love the land of Israel and seek the
settlement of the Holy Land for the same reason and holy goal that I have
in mind – because it is God's land, special and beloved out of the entire
world, containing unique holy qualities that foster prophesy and Divine
inspiration . . . then it would be certainly a great honor for every important
rabbi and Torah scholar and *tzaddik* to be such a Zionist. Even your honor
should find nothing objectionable in this form of Zionism.

To summarize the salient points in Rav Kook's views on Zionism:

- There are historical precedents for significant Jewish movements in
  which irreligious Jews played a major role.
- The special merits of *Eretz Yisrael* will elevate those who participate in
  its settlement and rebuilding.

- The original roots of Zionism are holy, going back to the disciples of the Gaon of Vilna and the Baal Shem Tov. Zionism must be returned to these authentic holy roots.
- The success of secular Zionism is due to its non-sectarian concern for the entire Jewish people, and it serves as a necessary correction for the imbalances caused by centuries of statelessness.

The Balfour Declaration[1]

IN 1916, AFTER being stranded in Switzerland for nearly two years due to the outbreak of World War I, Rav Kook was invited to occupy the rabbinic post of the Machzikei HaDat congregation in London. He accepted the position, but on condition that after the war he be allowed to return unhindered to *Eretz Yisrael*.

"Not many days passed," noted Rabbi Shimon Glitzenstein, his personal secretary in London, "when already an atmosphere of influence on all circles of Jewish life in this large and important community was formed. All recognized his extraordinary concern for the entire Jewish people."

While Rav Kook certainly did not plan to spend three years in London, he would later describe the momentous events of this period – events in which he took an active role – as a "revelation of the hand of God" (*Igrot HaRe'iyah* vol. III, p. 100).

❧ NATIONAL TREACHERY

Soon after his arrival, Rav Kook was forced to battle Jews who were working to undermine the Jewish people's hopes of national rebirth in the

---

[1] Adapted from *Mo'adei HaRe'iyah*, pp. 391–393; *Celebration of the Soul*, pp. 186–189. Additional material from *Encyclopedia of Religious Zionism* vol. 5, pp. 179–190.

land of Israel. Certain assimilated leaders of the British Jewish community, who considered themselves "Englishmen of the Mosaic faith," openly opposed the Zionist front. This powerful group, which included the staunchly anti-Zionist Lord Montagu,[2] had great influence on the British government due to their socio-economic and political standing. They publicly declared to the British government that the Jewish religion has no connection to Jewish nationalism, and that they opposed all plans to designate Palestine as the Jewish homeland.

In a public notice "in response to this national treachery," Rav Kook harshly condemned all those "who tear apart the Jewish soul," seeking to shatter the wondrous unity of Jewish religion and Jewish nationalism.

> The entire debate whether it is our national or our religious heritage that preserves and sustains us [as Jews] is a bitter mockery. The perfection of "You are one and Your Name is one, and who is like Your nation, Israel, one nation in the land"[3] is indivisible.

Rav Kook's statement described the cruel injustice perpetrated by the nations over the centuries, and demanded that they atone for their terrible crimes by returning *Eretz Yisrael* to the Jewish people and help establish an independent Jewish state. The letter was read in all British synagogues after the Sabbath Torah reading and made a deep impression. He then sent an additional letter urging the members of all British synagogues to immediately request that the British government "aid us in our demand to return to our holy land, as our eternal national home" (*Igrot HaRe'iyah* vol. III, pp. 107–114).

Rav Kook's efforts succeeded, and the spiteful letter written by the influential Jewish leaders was disregarded. The major British newspapers noted

---

2   Edwin Montagu (1879–1924), the only Jewish member of the British cabinet during World War I, termed Zionism "a mischievous political creed."

3   From the Sabbath afternoon liturgy. The prayer describes the Jewish people both in terms of their special connection to God as well as their nationhood in their own land.

the spontaneous protest, thus repairing the negative impression caused by the assimilationists.

During the parliamentary debates over authorizing a national Jewish home in Palestine, several parliament members raised the claims advanced by the Jewish assimilationists. Such a mandate, they insisted, is contrary to the spirit of Judaism. Then Mr. Kiley, a proponent of the declaration, stood up and asked, "Upon whom shall we rely to decide the religious aspect of this issue – upon Lord Montagu, or upon Rabbi Kook, the rabbi of Machzikei HaDat?"

❧ CONGRATULATING THE BRITISH NATION

After the Balfour Declaration was passed in 1917, the Jewish leaders held a large celebratory banquet in London, to which they invited lords, dignitaries, and members of Parliament. Speech after speech by Jewish communal and Zionist leaders thanked the British for their historic act. When Rav Kook was given the honor of speaking, he announced:

> I have come not only to thank the British nation, but even more, to congratulate it for the privilege of making this declaration. The Jewish nation is the "scholar" among the nations, the "people of the Book," a nation of prophets; and it is a great honor for any nation to aid it. I bless the British nation for having extended such honorable aid to the people of the Torah, so that they may return to their land and renew their homeland.

❧ A WONDROUS CHAIN OF EVENTS

Rav Kook saw in the national return of the Jewish people an overt revelation of the hand of God. How could one be blind to the Divine nature of this historical process? He later wrote:

> An imperviousness to God's intervention in history plagues our generation. A series of wondrous events has, and continues to take place before us. Yet blind eyes fail to see the hand of God, and deaf ears fail to hear the Divine call guiding history.
>
> This sequence of events began with the immigration of the disciples of

the Baal Shem Tov and the Vilna Gaon to *Eretz Yisrael*. They were followed by the awakening of the *Chibat Zion* movement and the establishment of the first settlements. The Zionism founded by Herzl, the settling of the land by the pioneers of the Second Aliyah, the Balfour Declaration, and the affirmation of the mandate in San Remo by the League of Nations – these are the latest developments.

Taken individually, each event may be explained in a rational manner. But when they are viewed together, we may discern a wondrous chain of complementary links created and guided by a Divine hand. As the prophet of redemption cried out: "Hear, O deaf, and look! O blind, that you may see!" (Isaiah 42:18).

"Who Are You, Great Mountain?"[1]

⋆ AN ASSEMBLY IN JERUSALEM

In the summer of 1923, the Jewish community held a festive service in the Rabbi Yehudah Hasid synagogue in Jerusalem's Old City. The country was then under the rule of the British Mandate, and community leaders organized an assembly of prayers and thanks to the British government in honor of King George V's birthday.

The general atmosphere in the country was, however, one of disappointment and even bitterness. The 1917 Balfour Declaration and the 1920 San Remo Conference had promised to establish a Jewish national home in Palestine, but the policy of the British Mandate in practice was a different story. In an attempt to appease the Arabs, the British White Paper of 1922 placed severe limits on Jewish immigration. Britain furthermore split Mandatory Palestine into two, excluding all lands east of the Jordan River from Jewish settlement.

Rav Kook was one of the speakers at the 1923 assembly. In order to raise the spirits of the Jews of *Eretz Yisrael* – and also remind the British

---

1   Adapted from *Mo'adei HaRe'iyah*, p. 403.

government of its promises to the Jewish people – he quoted from the week's *Haftarah* reading. He spoke about the prophecy of Zechariah, who lived at the time of a previous return to Zion, when the Jewish people returned from the Babylonian exile 2,500 years earlier.

ZECHARIAH'S WORDS OF ENCOURAGEMENT

There are many parallels between that era and our own time. The Jews returning from Babylonia were disillusioned and downhearted, and the foreign peoples whom the Babylonians had settled in the land created many difficulties. Zechariah sought to reassure the discouraged Jewish settlers.

> Who are you, great mountain? Before Zerubavel, you will be a flat plain!
> (Zechariah 4:7)

To what "great mountain" was the prophet speaking?

The path leading toward the fulfillment of God's promise to His people, the return to Zion, was endorsed by the mighty empire of those days – Persia. Cyrus, the king of Persia, had officially appointed Zerubavel to oversee the rebuilding of the Jewish community in the land of Israel. Zerubavel, a direct descendant of King Jehoiachin, the penultimate king of Judah, led the first band of Jews back to Jerusalem.

There were, however, many obstacles on the way. The prophet poetically refers to these hurdles as "great mountains," blocking the path and obstructing the return to Zion. Yet, before the king's representative, Zerubavel, these difficulties are nothing; he will flatten them like a level plain.

THE MISSION OF THE KING'S REPRESENTATIVE

We live in similar times, Rav Kook concluded. God is fulfilling His promise to restore the Jewish people to their land – this time, through the mighty empire of Great Britain. It is our expectation that, in accordance with the declaration of His Majesty's government, the king's representative – the British High Commissioner – will expedite the return of Israel to the Holy Land, despite the difficulties obstructing this historic process.

"*Who are you, great mountain?*" Regardless of the complexity of the problems, despite the desire of other peoples to hinder and obstruct, before the power of the tool of Divine Providence, all of these obstacles will be smoothed over and the path to redemption will be like "a level plain."

Redeeming the Land[1]

At a 1930 building dedication for the Jewish National Fund, the organization established to redeem land in Eretz Yisrael, Rav Kook spoke about the rights of the Jewish people to the land of Israel.

◌ RIGHTEOUS AND FAITHFUL

The prophet Isaiah proudly called out, "Open, O gates, so that the righteous nation that keeps faithfulness may enter" (26:2). Isaiah mentioned two qualities of the Jewish people:

- They "keep faithfulness" – i.e., they are loyal to their special covenant with God.
- They are a "righteous nation" – they act in a fair and just manner.

This attitude of fairness is expressed not only toward individuals. Also on the national level, in our relations with other peoples, we aspire to equitable dealings. Thus, even as we take the necessary steps toward reclaiming our land, we do so in a just and magnanimous fashion. As we return to the land of Israel, we eschew taking it by force, preferring to use peaceful

---

1   Adapted from *Mo'adei HaRe'iyah*, pp. 413–415.

methods, paying for property in full. We do this even though our rights to *Eretz Yisrael* were never abrogated.

✣ ETERNAL RIGHTS

Our eternal rights to the land of Israel have a firm basis in Jewish law. Rabbi Nachshon Gaon, the ninth-century head of the academy in Sura, wrote that any Jew can execute a legal transaction on the basis of land (*kinyan agav karka*).[2] This is true, the scholar explained, even if one does not own any real estate, since every Jew possesses a personal inheritance of four cubits in *Eretz Yisrael*. From here we see that even during those times when the land of Israel was stolen from us, this theft did not void our legal rights to the Land.

While there is a rule that "land cannot be stolen" (*Sukkah* 30b), it is likely that the conquest of land in war may be considered a form of acquisition that nullifies prior ownership of property. However, that is only true for land that the owners have the right to buy and sell. With regard to the land of Israel, the Torah states, "The land cannot be permanently sold, for the land is Mine" (Lev. 25:23). The special bond between the land of Israel and the Jewish people is enforced by a Divine right that may never be annulled. No form of acquisition, whether by purchase or conquest, can cancel a Jew's rights to his portion in the Land. And certainly nothing has the power to revoke the rights of the entire Jewish people to their holy inheritance.

✣ RECLAIMING THE LAND

However, since we are a "righteous nation," we try as much as possible to ensure that our redemption of the land of Israel be through consent, reclaiming the land with monetary acquisitions. In this way, the nations of the world cannot lodge complaints against us. As the Midrash states,

> Regarding three places, the nations of the world cannot claim, "You are occupying stolen territory," since they were purchased at full price. They

2   Quoted in the responsa of Rabbi Meir of Rothenburg (1215–1293).

are the *Machpeilah* cave in Hebron, the field in Shechem, and Mount Moriah in Jerusalem.[3] (*Breishit Rabbah* 79:7)

As we return to our homeland and renew our ownership of the land, we exercise both our eternal rights of Divine inheritance and also the accepted means of monetary acquisition. The JNF, which has proudly taken upon itself this historic mission of redeeming the Land, works to fulfill Isaiah's stirring call. May the gates of *Eretz Yisrael* open up, "so that the righteous nation that keeps faithfulness may enter!"

---

3   Abraham's purchase of the *Machpeilah* cave is recorded in Gen. 23, Jacob's purchase of a field in Shechem in Gen. 33:19, and David's purchase of Mount Moriah in II Sam. 24:24.

The Sanctity of Yom Ha'Atzmaut[1]

I S THERE MORE to Israel Independence Day than just fireworks and flag-waving? Is Yom Ha'Atzmaut just a secular holiday commemorating our political independence, or does it hold a deeper meaning for us?

❧ THE HOLINESS OF MITZVOT

Rav Kook passed away in 1935, thirteen years before the State of Israel was established, but his son Rav Tzvi Yehudah Kook interpreted the historic events of 1948 in light of his father's teachings. In an article entitled "Affirming the Sanctity of the Day of Our Independence," Rav Tzvi Yehudah analyzed the religious significance of Yom Ha'Atzmaut.

In general, our connection to sanctity and holiness is through the mitzvot of the Torah. Thus before performing a mitzvah we say, "Who sanctified us with His mitzvot." The holiness of Yom Ha'Atzmaut, Rav Tzvi Yehudah explained, is anchored in the holiness of mitzvot. But which particular mitzvah is connected to this historical occasion?

The Ramban[2] defined the mitzvah of *yishuv ha'aretz*, settling the land of

---

1 Adapted from *LeNetivot Yisrael* vol. I, pp. 181–184, 192–200, and *Sichot HaRav Tzvi Yehudah* 19.
2 Rabbi Moshe ben Nachman (Nachmanides) of Gerona, Spain (1194–1270). The Ramban

Israel, as "we will not abandon it to another nation, or leave it desolate." This definition makes it clear that the mitzvah is first and foremost an obligation of the nation; the Jewish people are commanded to take possession of the land of Israel and rule over it. On the basis of that national mitzvah, there is a mitzvah for each individual to live in *Eretz Yisrael*.

The Ramban emphasized that this mitzvah is in effect at all times. This view is upheld in the *Shulchan Aruch* (*Even Ha'ezer* 75:6, *Pitchei Teshuvah* ad loc).

This then is the significance of Yom Ha'Atzmaut: that we have finally merited, after centuries of exile, to once again fulfill this lofty mitzvah, valued by the Sages as "equal to all the other mitzvot" (*Sifre Re'eih*), "to return and possess the land that God promised to our fathers" (Ramban). We should be full of gratitude to live here, in *Eretz Yisrael*, "the place that Moses and Aaron did not merit" (*Ketubot* 112a). We should be grateful to be alive at this time in history, to witness the hour of redemption that so many great and holy leaders of our people did not merit to see.

❧ COURAGEOUS SPIRIT

And yet one may ask: why should the fifth day of Iyyar be chosen for celebrating this event? Perhaps a different date, such as the date of the cease-fire after the War of Independence, would be a more appropriate choice?

While the military victory of a fledgling state over the armies of five enemy countries was certainly miraculous, that was *not* the greatest miracle of the establishment of the State of Israel. The true miracle was the remarkable courage displayed on the fifth of Iyyar in making the fateful decision and announcing the establishment of an independent state. This decision, in the face of heavy pressure from the U.S. State Department not to declare a state, and belligerent threats of the surrounding Arab countries to attack and destroy the Jewish community in *Eretz Yisrael*, was by no means a trivial

---

wrote this definition of *yishuv ha'aretz* in his appendix to Maimonides' *Sefer Hamitzvot*, positive mitzvah #4.

matter. The motion to declare a state passed by only a thin majority in Ben-Gurion's cabinet.[3]

This courageous decision was the true miracle of Yom Ha'Atzmaut. The Talmud in *Baba Metzia* 106a states that a shepherd's rescue of his flock from a lion or a bear may be considered a miracle. Where exactly is the miracle in this act? The Tosafists explained that the miracle is to be found in the shepherd's "spirit of courage and willingness to fight." This spirit of valor is a miracle from above, an inspired inner greatness spurring one to rise to the needs of the hour. This is the significance of Ezekiel's prophetic description of the redemption:

> I will place My spirit in you and you shall live. I will set you on your land, and you will know that I, the Eternal, have spoken and performed it.
>
> (Ezekiel 37:14)

❧ ATCHALTA DEGEULAH

Nevertheless, many people have difficulty reconciling the current moral and spiritual state of Israel with the vision of the redemption as portrayed by the prophets and the sages. Is this the Messianic Era for which we prayed two thousand years?

The Sages determined that "The only difference between the current reality and the Messianic Era is [independence from] the rule of foreign powers" (*Berachot* 34b; *Mishneh Torah*, Laws of Kings 12:2). While we have certainly not yet merited the final phase of redemption, we *have* achieved this criterion of redemption – independence and self-rule over our geographical area.

Many Torah scholars fought against the Zionist movement because they envisioned redemption as a future era that arrives complete from the very

---

3   One of the signers to the Declaration of Independence, Moshe Sharett, later recalled in his diary how he had signed with "a sense of excitement together with a clear premonition of danger, such as one might feel while standing on a cliff, ready to leap into a yawning chasm. We felt as though we stood on a very high crest, where roaring winds were brewing about us, and that we had to stand fast."

start, and not an ongoing process. But the import of the Talmudic statement (Jer. *Berachot* 1:1) that the redemption will appear "little by little," like the spreading light of dawn in the morning sky, is exactly this: that the redemption is a process that advances in stages.

We need to examine history with a perspective of faith in God. We need to recognize that the Master of the universe controls and governs all events. The Sages taught:

> What is the meaning of the verse, "For who has scorned the day of smallness" (Zecharia 4:10)? What causes the table of the righteous to be scorned in the future era? Their smallness of faith, that they failed to believe in the Holy One. (*Sotah* 48b)

Why is the future portion (the "table") of the *tzadikim* marred? Because they are *tzadikim* who lack faith in God. They view the world with a narrow outlook, and fail to see God's hand in the events of history. The redemption does not have to come through great miracles; God can also bring the redemption using natural forces and events.

❧ EZEKIEL'S PROPHECY OF REDEMPTION

The various stages of redemption are clearly described in the order of events in Ezekiel's prophecy. The prophecy first speaks of the initial stage of redemption, the ingathering of the exiles:

> I will take you from the nations and gather you from all the lands, and I will bring you to your land. (36:24)

Only after this initial redemption does the prophet describe the spiritual return and *teshuvah* of the people:

> I will sprinkle over you purifying water and you will be purified from all of your impurities .... I will give you a new heart, and a new spirit I will place in you. I will remove the heart of stone from your flesh and give you a heart of flesh. I will put My spirit within you so that you will

walk in My statutes . . . . And you will be My people, and I will be your God. (36:25–28)

This narrative of the redemption concurs with the opinion of Rabbi Joshua in *Sanhedrin* 97b, that the redemption will come regardless of the merits of the Jewish people – "even if they do not repent."[4]

---

4 See *LeNetivot Yisrael*, pp. 195–196, where Rav Tzvi Yehudah Kook demonstrates that the Halachah follows this opinion.

LAG BA'OMER[1]

ל"ג בעומר

A Time for Esoteric Wisdom

When the world functions in its normal fashion, when there are no disturbances and upheavals in life, then even one's lofty ideas may be cultivated by observing the patterns of life, social living, and the corresponding areas of Torah. This is the essence of all revealed wisdom and learning. One is assured of gaining inner wealth from these assets.

But all this changes when life descends into the chasms of dark cruelty and destruction. Then the ordinary world staggers, its regular order confused. [At such times,] were one to derive the marrow of his spiritual life only from the revealed side of the treasury of the spirit, he would be subject to a terrible atrophy, stripping him of his state of moral purity. In order to maintain one's [spiritual] level, a burning thirst for the hidden content, for the inner perceptions that transcend the revealed view of life, is awakened. This is an area undisturbed by world upheaval. From this [esoteric] source of life one may "draw water in joy,"[2] reviving the dry bones of the revealed spiritual realm that was so jolted by the violence of a chaotic world.[3]

(*Rosh Millin*, p. 136, *Mo'adei HaRe'iyah*, p. 460)

---

1   Lag Ba'Omer – the 33rd day from the Omer offering – commemorates the day when the plague killing Rabbi Akiva's students ceased, and the passing of famed second-century mystic Rabbi Shimon bar Yochai, author of the Zohar.

2   Isaiah 12:3. Rav Kook is alluding to the verse's Aramaic translation (Targum Yonatan): "You will receive a new teaching from the most chosen among the righteous."

3   This passage reflects on the Zohar's origin in the years that Rabbi Shimon bar Yochai hid in a cave, a fugitive of Roman persecution. Rabbi Shimon's immersion in esoteric studies, Rav Kook explained, was due to the chaotic nature of Jewish life at that time, as Roman persecution lead to revolt and exile. The quote itself is taken from *Rosh Millin*, Rav Kook's most explicitly Kabbalistic work, written in England during the terrible upheavals of World War 1. Rav Kook concluded the passage by noting, "It is for this reason that the author of these lines felt compelled to record these thoughts about the esoteric significance of the Hebrew letters, etc. at this particular time."

Elevated Souls[1]

T HE TALMUD IN *Sukkah* 45b records the following pronouncement
by the great mystic Rabbi Shimon bar Yochai:

> I have seen people of high attainments (*bnei aliyah*), but they are few. If
> there are a thousand, then I and my son are among them. If there are a
> hundred, then I and my son are among them. And if there are only two,
> then they are me and my son.

How could Rabbi Shimon make such a bold – even boastful – claim?

❧ LOST IN JAFFA

Rav Kook, who was often immersed in deep reflections, was not an
expert in the streets and pathways of Jaffa. Once he went for a walk with
Rabbi Zalman Shach, assuming that his companion knew the way. Soon it
became apparent that Rabbi Shach was also unfamiliar with the area, and
the two scholars realized that they were lost. How did they find their way
back? Rav Kook hid in a nearby courtyard while Rabbi Shach stopped a
child and asked him where Rav Kook lived. After the boy described where

---

1   Adapted from *Mo'adei HaRe'iyah*, pp. 81, 431; *Arpilei Tohar* (Shilat edition), p. 111.

to go, Rabbi Shach waited until he had left, approached Rav Kook, and together they returned home.[2]

During his later years in Jerusalem, Rav Kook would spend short summer vacations in the quiet neighborhood of Kiryat Moshe. One evening, Rabbi Yitzchak Hutner, whom Rav Kook greatly favored, came to visit. The Rav went on a short walk with his young guest. Remembering what had happened in Jaffa, he asked his companion whether he knew the area; otherwise, he suggested, it would be best not to stray too far from the house, so they would not need to ask for directions.

Rabbi Hutner responded, "I am sure that if the Holy Temple were built and you were officiating as the High Priest, you would know every entrance and passageway of the Temple."

Rav Kook considered this comment and humbly agreed. "Yes. With holy matters, one remembers."

༃ LIVING IN THE UPPER REALM

Rav Kook gave an original interpretation for Rabbi Shimon bar Yochai's expression, *bnei aliyah*. One meaning of the word *aliyah* is "upper floor" or "attic."[3] The *bnei aliyah* are those lofty souls who live in the "upper floor" of reality. Their point of reference is the spiritual world, and in order to understand the physical world – the bottom floor – they must lower their sights.

The vast majority of people are firmly entrenched in this world. Their point of reference is the physical realm. For them, comprehending the spiritual reality requires intense intellectual effort; they need examples and allegories based on the physical world in order to understand spiritual truths.

---

2   Not long after this incident, an article appeared praising Rav Kook's erudition. The writer, who wanted to describe the Rav's expertise in both the Babylonian and Jerusalem Talmuds, paraphrased a Talmudic phrase and wrote that "The paths of the Jerusalem [Talmud] are as clear to him as the streets of Jaffa." Rav Kook smiled when he heard about the article. "Woe to me," he wryly observed, "if I were to know the Jerusalem Talmud the way I know the streets of Jaffa!"

3   See, for example, II Kings 4:10 – "Let us make a small walled upper chamber [*aliyat-kir*]."

For the *bnei aliyah*, however, it is just the opposite. These elevated souls truly live in the spiritual realm. Understanding the workings of that elevated reality comes naturally to them, while relating to the physical world requires a measure of intellectual effort.

Thus Rabbi Shimon bar Yochai was simply reflecting on the basic orientation of his soul. He and his son were *bnei aliyah*, at home in the higher spiritual dimension. And it was from that elevated perspective that they viewed the physical world.

Rabbi Shimon bar Yochai Returns[1]

With the death of the Roman emperor, Rabbi Shimon bar Yochai could finally leave the cave where he and his son had hidden for thirteen years, studying Torah as they lay buried in the sand. But the long years of deprivation and harsh physical conditions had taken a terrible toll on Rabbi Shimon's body.

The Talmud in *Shabbat* 33b relates that Rabbi Shimon's son-in-law, Rabbi Pinchas ben Yair, went to greet them. Rabbi Pinchas brought his father-in-law to the bathhouse and treated his skin. When Rabbi Pinchas saw the deep cuts in Rabbi Shimon's skin, he began to weep. His salty tears fell onto Rabbi Shimon – and Rabbi Shimon cried out from the pain.

"Woe is me to have seen you in such a state," Rabbi Pinchas lamented.

"On the contrary, you are fortunate to have seen me so," replied Rabbi Shimon. *"For if you had not seen me so, you would not have found in me that which you have found."*

What did Rabbi Shimon mean by this response? What benefit was there in the scholar's deteriorated state of health?

---

1   Adapted from *Ein Ayah* vol. III to *Shabbat* 33b (2:281).

❧ STRENGTH TO TEACH

A holy *tzaddik* like Rabbi Shimon, completely detached from the material world, gave little notice to his physical state. His uniquely elevated soul found comfort and joy in the light of a higher realm, a supernal light that alleviates all physical pain and suffering.

However, Rabbi Shimon's ability to teach and influence others was certainly limited by his physical weakness and ill health. For this reason, Rabbi Pinchas cried when he saw his father-in-law's physical state. "Woe is me to have seen you in such a state!"

❧ A HIGHER WISDOM TO IMPART

Rabbi Shimon, however, disagreed with this assessment. Rabbi Shimon understood that, on the contrary, it was only due to his current state that he would be able to truly accomplish his mission.

The holy *tzaddik* was appalled by the widespread materialism and crassness in the world around him. The Talmud relates that when Rabbi Shimon and his son first left the cave, everywhere they looked was immediately consumed by fire. They could not reconcile themselves to society's obsession with worldly matters. "They forsake eternal life and engage in temporal life!" they exclaimed.

If I wish to raise up those mired in the depths of materialism, Rabbi Shimon reasoned, I must first gain for myself a complete mastery over physical desires and transient matters.

Rabbi Pinchas realized that his father-in-law was only able to attain his unique spiritual level by neglecting his body during those long years of concentrated study and prayer in the cave. But Rabbi Pinchas failed to recognize that, beyond Rabbi Shimon's own personal spiritual growth, this period also prepared him to influence others on a deeper level. Rabbi Shimon therefore explained to him, "You are fortunate to have seen me so." Also for your sakes, it is good that I am the way I am. Now you will be able to gain far greater benefit from me. Now you will find in me a higher and more profound wisdom.

Rabbi Shimon's response is now clear. "If you had not seen me so, you would not have found in me that which you have found." Even "that which you find in me" – even my ability to teach and enlighten you – is enhanced according to the quality of my soul's inner purity, an inner aspect not bound by my abilities to communicate with others. The degree by which we are able to influence others is not only a function of rhetoric and eloquence. The extent of our influence primarily depends on an inner quality beyond words and language, a quality residing in the inner chambers of the soul.

The Talmud confirmed Rabbi Shimon's insight with a simple empirical observation. Before he entered the cave, Rabbi Shimon would pose a question and Rabbi Pinchas would offer twelve solutions. After he left the cave, however, Rabbi Pinchas would be the one raising the question. And Rabbi Shimon's enhanced wisdom was such that he would respond, not with twelve solutions, but with twenty-four.

The Torah of Rashbi[1]

AMAZINGLY ENOUGH, NOT everyone needs to pray:

> Those whose full-time occupation is learning Torah, such as Rabbi Shimon Bar Yochai and his colleagues, should interrupt their studies to recite the *Shema* but not for the *Amidah* prayer. (*Shulchan Aruch Orach Chaim* 106:2, based on *Shabbat* 11a)

This statement is quite surprising. Does not prayer fulfill a basic spiritual need? True, Rabbi Shimon bar Yochai was a great scholar who completely immersed himself in Torah study – but why should he be exempt from prayer?

Rav Kook's explanation in *Olat Re'iyah* helps us understand the function of prayer and the mechanics of its role in our spiritual growth.

THEORETICAL AND PRACTICAL

The Sages used an interesting phrase to describe full-time Torah scholars: "their Torah is their *umanut*" – their art or craft. In what way is Torah study likened to a craft?

A craft is a skill based on specialized wisdom and knowledge. However, it is not enough just to learn the theory. The craftsman also needs practical training in order to perfect his art.

[1] Adapted from *Olat Re'iyah*, introduction to vol. I, pp. 21–22.

However, there are unusual individuals who are so talented that they fall under the category of one who "just sees an art and acquires the skill." Using only their mental powers, they are able to acquire the necessary practical skill. One example of such a gifted artist was Betzalel. He was blessed with a unique Divine spirit that enabled him to create all of the beautiful and intricate Tabernacle vessels solely on the basis of their theoretical specifications, without needing to resort to apprenticeship and experimentation.

·δ· THE ART OF TORAH

The Torah may also be described as a theoretical wisdom that needs to be actualized on a practical level. It is not enough just to study about kindness and integrity and holiness. The basis for our good deeds and holy service is when we succeed in integrating the highest perceptions of Divine ideals into our lives.

It is precisely in this transformation from theory to practice that prayer plays a crucial role. Prayer reaches out to our emotions and feelings. Because emotions have a stronger impact on actions than abstract thought, prayer enables us to realize our ethical principles in our day-to-day lives. Our prayers for enlightenment, forgiveness, redemption, and so on, awaken deep yearnings for these eternal values. Prayer softens the heart and prepares us to actualize those concepts of morality and holiness acquired in Torah study. Earnest prayer prepares us to become skilled artists of kindness and integrity.

Rabbi Shimon bar Yochai, however, was a special case. His absorption of Torah was profound and all-encompassing. The impact of his Torah studies was so powerful, and he was so innately attuned to internalize every teaching of holiness and goodness, that he did not need prayer in order to refine his emotions. His Torah study alone was enough to stamp its spiritual images deeply on his heart and soul. He was like the gifted individual who "just sees an art and acquires the skill." Rabbi Shimon was gifted in his Torah study like Betzalel was blessed in his craftsmanship.

For this reason, Rabbi Shimon bar Yochai and scholars like him are exempt from prayer. Their Torah study alone is enough to serve as the foundation for the practical application of their "craft."

JERUSALEM DAY [1]
יום ירושלים

The Call of the Nation's Soul

Our ancient oath was for the sake of Jerusalem – "If I will forget you, Jerusalem, let my right hand forget its skill" (Ps. 137:5). Twice each year, a voice accompanies us in the majesty of its hope: on the holy eve of the Passover holiday, and at the conclusion of the holiest day [Yom Kippur]. This is the voice of the nation's soul, as it calls out the depths of its yearnings and anticipated longing: "Next year in Jerusalem!"

(Mo'adei HaRe'iyah, p. 463)

1   Jerusalem Day is a national holiday on the 28th of Iyyar, celebrating the liberation of the Old City of Jerusalem and its reunification in June 1967.

The Two Messengers[1]

T HE PROPHET ISAIAH used a metaphor of two messengers, the Herald of Zion and the Herald of Jerusalem, who together proclaim the imminent redemption of Israel:

עַל הַר גָּבֹהַּ עֲלִי־לָךְ, מְבַשֶּׂרֶת צִיּוֹן. הָרִימִי בַכֹּחַ קוֹלֵךְ, מְבַשֶּׂרֶת יְרוּשָׁלָם. (ישעיהו מ:ט)

Herald of Zion, ascend a lofty mountain!
Herald of Jerusalem, lift up your voice with strength, be not afraid! (Is. 40:9)

Who are these two messengers? Why was one commanded to scale the mountain, while the second messenger was instructed to raise her voice?

ZION AND JERUSALEM

We must first analyze the difference between the names "Zion" and "Jerusalem." "Zion" represents our national aspirations for autonomy and independence, while "Jerusalem" symbolizes our lofty visions for holiness and spiritual greatness. The Herald of Zion is none other than the Zionist movement, demanding the restoration of independence and sovereignty for

---

1   Adapted from *Mo'adei HaRe'iyah,* pp. 482–483.

the Jewish people in their own land. This call is heard clearly around the world; there is no need to further raise its voice.

However, secular Zionism is only concerned with our legitimate rights to self-rule. Its aspirations are the same as those of every other nation.

The Herald of Jerusalem, on the other hand, speaks of our return to holiness, so that we may fulfill our national destiny as "a kingdom of priests and a holy nation" (Ex. 19:6). This messenger of redemption calls for the restoration of Jerusalem, our holy city, and the holy Temple. Unlike the Herald of Zion, she stands on "a high mountain" – her vision comes from a high and lofty standpoint. But her voice is faint and her demand is not heard clearly. The Herald of Jerusalem seems to fear raising her voice too loudly.

The prophet found fault with both messengers. He reproved the Herald of Zion: Why are you standing down below, together with all the other nations? Why do you only speak of the commonplace goals of the gentile nations? "*Ascend a lofty mountain*!" Speak in the Name of God, in the name of Israel's holy mission, in the name of the prophetic visions of redemption for the Jewish people and all of humanity.

The prophet then turned to the Herald of Jerusalem: You who call for the return to the city of holiness, you are speaking from the right place, demanding our lofty ideals. But your voice is not heard. You need to learn from the Herald of Zion and "*Lift up your voice in strength, be not afraid!*"

Windows to the City of Peace[1]

O VER THE MILLENNIA, Jews have faced the holy city of Jerusalem
when praying. The Talmud in *Berachot* 34b derives this practice
from how Daniel would pray in Babylon:

> One should only pray in a house which has windows, as it says, "And
> Daniel would enter his house, where there were open windows in his
> upper chamber facing Jerusalem; three times a day he would kneel and
> pray" (Daniel 6:11).

Why are windows needed for prayer? Is not prayer a private exercise
of the soul, where one concentrates inward? And why did Daniel have his
windows facing Jerusalem?

ENGAGED PRAYER

Prayer is an intensely introspective activity, but it should not lead us to
belittle the value of being part of the world around us. If meditation and
private prayer lead us to withdraw from the outside world, then we have
missed prayer's ultimate goal. The full import of prayer cannot be properly
realized by those secluded in a monastery, cut off from the world. Prayer

---

1   Adapted from *Ein Ayah* vol. I on *Berachot* 34b (5:124).

should inspire us to take action for just and worthy causes. For this reason, the Sages taught that we should pray in a room with windows, thus indicating our ties and moral obligations to the greater world.

As we affirm our connection to the world, it is important that we turn toward the city of Jerusalem. Our aspirations for perfecting the world should be channeled through the goal of universal peace. This is the significance of directing our prayers toward Jerusalem, whose name means "the city of peace." Jerusalem is the focal point from which God's prophetic message emanates to the world – "For the Torah shall come forth from Zion, and God's word from Jerusalem" (Isaiah 2:3).

Zion and Jerusalem[1]

❧ A WARNING FROM *ERETZ YISRAEL*

The sages in *Eretz Yisrael* were furious. True, Hananiah was a great scholar, among the greatest of his generation. But even after he left for Babylon,[2] Hananiah continued to set the Jewish calendar, deciding whether to add a leap month and determining the first day of the month.

The sages dispatched two messengers to Hananiah with the following warning: "If you insist on setting the calendar outside of Israel, then go build your own altar and publicly declare that you and your community in Babylon have left the Jewish people and no longer belong to the God of Israel." The Babylonian Jews were stunned to hear this message, wailing, "Heaven forbid! We are still part of the Jewish people!"

Why were the sages so disturbed by Hananiah's setting the calendar in Babylon? The Talmud (*Berachot* 63b) explains that their response was based on the verse, "For Torah will go forth out of Zion, and God's word from

---

1 Adapted from *Ein Ayah* vol. II on *Berachot* 63b (9:330).
2 Hananiah, a scholar of the second century, left the land of Israel for Babylonia due to the Hadrianic persecutions that followed the Bar Kochbah rebellion (*The Jewish Encyclopedia*, p. 207).

Jerusalem" (Isaiah 2:3). The source of Torah – including determining the Jewish calendar – is Jerusalem and the land of Israel. Why is it so important that Jerusalem be the center of Torah instruction?

ZION AND JERUSALEM

We must first understand this verse, "For Torah will go forth out of Zion, and God's word from Jerusalem." What is the difference between "Zion" and "Jerusalem"?

While Zion and Jerusalem refer to the same locale, they indicate different aspects of the holy city. The word "Zion" literally means "marked" or "distinctive." It refers to those inner qualities that distinguish the Jewish people, "a nation who dwells alone" (Num. 23:9) with their own unique spiritual traits and aspirations. The name "Jerusalem," on the other hand, indicates the city's function as a spiritual center for the entire world, influencing the nations of the world. "Jerusalem" is the means by which Israel's spirit of holiness penetrates and uplifts the inner life of distant peoples.

In short, "Zion" looks inward, emphasizing the city's internal significance for the Jewish people, while "Jerusalem" looks outward, stressing the city's universal role as a spiritual focal point for the world.

It is axiomatic that the spirit of Torah and its ideals can only flourish when the Jewish people observe the Torah's mitzvot. For this reason, the verse first stipulates that "Torah will go forth out of Zion." First the Jewish people must follow Torah and its mitzvot; only then can God's word disseminate from Jerusalem to the rest of the world. The two parts of the verse thus correspond to the dual aspects of Zion-Jerusalem. First there must be Torah in Zion, focusing inward. Then "the word of God" – the universal prophetic message – can spread to the rest of the world, emanating from "Jerusalem," the international quality of the holy city.

THE SUN AND THE MOON

What does all of this have to do with setting the calendar? There are two aspects to setting the Jewish calendar. The first is to determine the hour of the new moon, and the second is to calculate whether it is necessary to intercalate an extra month so that the lunar cycle will remain in sync with the solar year and the seasons.

In rabbinical literature, the sun is often a metaphor for the nations of the world, while the moon represents the Jewish people. Thus the two calculations of the calendar correspond to the two aspects of Zion-Jerusalem. We need to determine the time of the new moon in order to observe the special lunar calendar of Israel – this is the internal Torah of Zion. And we need to declare a leap year in order to maintain the proper balance between the lunar year of Israel and the solar year of the nations – this corresponds to the universal message emanating from Jerusalem.

ᴸ THE TORAH OF A NATION

But why must the Jewish calendar be set in the land of Israel? The restriction on setting the calendar in *Eretz Yisrael* reflects a fundamental axiom of Torah. For the Torah to influence and enlighten the world, it must be established as a complete Torah, a Torah that governs all spheres of life. By setting the calendar outside of Israel, Hananiah disconnected the Torah from the myriad aspects of life as a nation living in its own land. He reduced the Torah to a personal religion that only relates to the ethical refinement of the individual and one's private connection to God. Such an approach impoverishes the multifaceted richness of Torah. As the sages warned Hananiah, this was akin to setting up a private altar to serve God – an irreparable break from the true goal of Torah and the people of Israel.

To thwart such misguided views, the prophet declared, "For the sake of Zion I will not be silent" (Isaiah 62:1). First, Zion's status as the center of Torah must be firmly established. Only then will the continuation of this prophecy be fulfilled: "Then the nations will see your righteousness, and all kingdoms your honor."

SHAVUOT
שבועות

Introducing Infinite Light into a Finite World

The Torah was given to the world in order to introduce all of the elevated light – a light transcending all aims and objectives – into the limited universe, a realm paved with goals and intentions, restrictions and boundaries, to enlighten all of its darkness with its holy splendor.

The light of Torah bursts forth from the heights of eternity. It penetrates the deepest depths, the smallest crevices of the most minute aspects of creation, all hidden facets of life. [This light] binds together all of reality from beginning to end, elevating it for all time.

(*Olat Re'iyah* vol. 1, p. 185; *Mo'adei HaRe'iyah*, p. 485)

Seeing Sound[1]

And all the people *saw the sounds* .... (Ex. 20:14)

THE MIDRASH CALLS our attention to an amazing aspect of the revelation at Sinai: the Jewish people were able to see what is normally only heard. What does this mean?

ॐ STANDING NEAR THE SOURCE

At their source, sound and sight are united. Only in our limited, physical world, in this *alma deperuda* (disjointed world), are these phenomena disconnected and detached. This is similar to our perception of lightning and thunder, which become increasingly separated from one another as the observer is more distanced from the source.

If we are bound and limited to the present, if we can only perceive the universe through the viewpoint of the temporal and the material, then we will always be aware of the divide between sight and sound. The prophetic vision at Mount Sinai, however, granted the people a unique perspective, as if they were standing near the source of Creation. From that vantage point, they were able to witness the underlying unity of the universe. They were able to see sounds and hear sights. God's revelation at Sinai was registered by all their senses simultaneously, as a single, undivided perception.

[1] Adapted from *Mo'adei HaRe'iyah*, p. 491.

꙳

The King's Torah Scroll[1]

W HILE THE TORAH commands every Jew to write a Torah
scroll,[2] there is one individual who is obligated to write an
additional Torah scroll. Surprisingly, it is neither the high
priest, nor the head of Sanhedrin. It is the *king* who is commanded to write a
second Torah scroll during his reign and keep it with him at all times (Deut.
17:18–19, *Sanhedrin* 2:4).

What is the significance of these two Torah scrolls, that of the individual
and that of the king?

꙳ PERSONAL TORAH AND COMMUNAL TORAH

The people of Israel accepted the Torah at Sinai on two levels. Each
individual consented to follow the Torah's laws as a member of the Jewish
people. And the Jewish people as a nation also accepted the Torah, so that

---

1 Adapted from *Ma'amarei HaRe'iyah*, pp. 173–174.
2 *Sanhedrin* 91b, based on Deut. 31:19. However, the *Shulchan Aruch* (*Yoreh Dei'ah* 270:2)
quotes the opinion of Rabbeinu Asher (the *Rosh*), that "nowadays it is a mitzvah to write
books of the Pentateuch, Mishnah, Talmud, and their commentaries," since we no longer
study directly from Torah scrolls. (The authorities debate whether there is still a mitzvah
to write a Torah scroll, see *Shach* and *Taz* ad loc.)

its moral instructions are binding on its national institutions – the judiciary, the government, the army, and so on.

Observing the Torah on the national level is, however, far more complex than the individual's observance of the Torah. The Torah and its mitzvot were given to refine and elevate humanity. The process of uplifting an entire nation, with its political exigencies and security needs, is far more complicated than the process of elevating the individual.

As individuals, we approach issues of interpersonal morality informed by an innate sense of justice. Mankind, however, has yet to attain a consensus on the ethical issues connected to affairs of state. Furthermore, the propensity for moral lapse – and the severity of such lapses – is far greater on the national level. As a result, all notions of good and evil, propriety and injustice, are frequently lost amidst the raging turmoil of political issues and national concerns.

The greatness of the messianic king lies in his potential to fulfill the Torah's ethical ideals also in the political realm. We read about the foundation of the messianic dynasty in the book of Ruth, which concludes with the lineage of David, king of Israel. Why is it customary to read the book of Ruth on the holiday of Shavuot? Because the account of the origins of the Davidic dynasty reminds us of the second level of Torah law that we accepted at Sinai, that of the nation as a whole.

Rav Kook cautioned regarding the moral and spiritual dangers inherent in political life:

> We must not allow the tendency toward factionalism, which threatens most strongly at the inception of a political movement, to deter us from seeking justice and truth, from loving all of humanity, both the collective and the individual, from love for the Jewish people, and from the holy obligations that are unique to Israel. We are commanded not only to be holy individuals, but also, and especially, to be "a kingdom of priests and a holy nation."

Revealing Our Inner Essence[1]

Ｔ<small>HE ULTIMATE MOMENT</small> of glory for the Jewish people – their greatest hour – occurred as God revealed His Torah at Mount Sinai. The Israelites remarkably pledged, *Naaseh VeNishma* – "We will do and we will listen to all that God has declared" (Ex. 24:7).

They made two promises: to do, and to listen. The order is crucial. They promised to keep the Torah, even before knowing why. The Midrash (*Shabbat* 88a) relates that, in merit of this pledge of loyalty, the angels rewarded each Jew with two crowns. And a Heavenly Voice exclaimed, "Who revealed to My children this secret used by the angels?"

What was so special about this vow, "We will do and we will listen"? On the contrary, would not fulfilling mitzvot with understanding and enlightenment be a superior level of Torah observance? And why does the Midrash refer to this form of unquestioning allegiance as a "secret used by the angels"?

ᴔ INTUITIVE KNOWLEDGE

While wisdom is usually acquired through study and contemplation, there exists in nature an intuitive knowledge that requires no formal

[1] Adapted from *Mo'adei HaRe'iyah,* p. 486.

education. The bee, for example, naturally knows the optimal geometric shape for building honeycomb cells. No bee has ever needed to register for engineering courses at MIT.

Intuitive knowledge also exists in the spiritual realm. Angels are sublime spiritual entities who do not require extensive Torah study in order to know how to serve God. Their holiness is ingrained in their very nature. It is only human beings, prone to being confused by pseudo-scientific indoctrination, who need to struggle in order to return to their pristine spiritual selves.

For the Jews who stood at Mount Sinai, it was not only Torah and mitzvot that were revealed. They also discovered their own true, inner essence. They attained a sublime level of natural purity, and intuitively proclaimed, "We will do." We will follow our natural essence, unhindered by any spurious, artificial conventions.

The Date of Matan Torah[1]

O N WHAT DAY was the Torah revealed to Israel? The majority
opinion is that the Torah was given on the sixth day of Sivan.
Rabbi Yossi, however, disagreed, arguing that the Torah was given
on the seventh of Sivan (*Shabbat* 86b).

What is the essence of this disagreement? What is the significance of the
date of *Matan Torah*?

﹖ PERFECTING CREATION

Rav Kook explained that the Sages were debating the fundamental goal
of the Torah. The sixth and seventh of Sivan correspond to the very first
sixth and seventh days in history – the sixth and seventh day of Creation.

Most of the Sages associated the Siniatic revelation with the sixth day of
Creation, the day that mankind was created. This connection indicates that
the primary objective of the Torah is to complete that act of Creation – the
birth of humanity. The goal of Torah is to perfect humanity, to recreate it in
a holier, purer form.

Rabbi Yossi, on the other hand, wanted to stress an even higher goal of
the Torah. For after the Torah has made its mark on mankind and its ideals

---

1   Adapted from *Ein Ayah* vol. IV on *Shabbat* 86b (9:17).

have been internalized in the human heart, it will then take root into the innermost soul of the world, uplifting and refining the entire universe.

In terms of this ultimate goal of the Torah, it is fitting that the Torah be revealed to the world on the seventh day, the concluding day of Creation. Through the seventh day, the Torah is linked to the true culmination of Creation – the Sabbath, the day of ultimate perfection and rest.

Accepting Two Torahs[1]

A CAREFUL READING OF the Torah's account of *Matan Torah* indicates that the Jewish people accepted the Torah not once but twice. First it says:

> Moses came and told the people all of God's words and all of the laws. The entire people responded with a single voice, "All the words that God spoke – we will do [*Na'aseh*]." (Ex. 24:3)

Immediately afterward, we read:

> Moses wrote down all of God's words. ... He took the book of the covenant and read it to the people. They responded, "All that God said, we will do and we will understand[2] [*Na'aseh VeNishma*]." (Ex. 24:4, 7)

These two passages cannot refer to the same event. In the first account, Moses communicated God's words orally, while in the second account he read to the people from *sefer habrit*, the written record of God's word.

---

1   Adapted from *Midbar Shur*, pp. 160–165.
2   The word *nishma* literally means "we will hear." While this could be taken to mean "we will obey," the Talmud in *Shabbat* 88a interprets *nishma* to mean "we will understand." (See Gen. 42:23 and Deut. 28:49, where the root *shama* can only carry the meaning "to understand.")

This corresponds to the teaching of the Sages that not one but two Torahs were given at Mount Sinai – the Oral Law and the Written Law. The Jewish people first accepted upon themselves the Oral Torah, and afterward, the Written Torah.

ঙ WHY TWO TORAHS?

Why was it necessary for the Torah to be given both orally and in writing? And why did the people accept the Oral Torah with the words, "We will do," but when accepting the Written Torah they added, "and we will understand"?

There are two aspects to Torah study. The primary goal of Torah is to know how we should conduct ourselves. This is the function of the Oral Law – the Mishnah and the Talmud – which discusses in detail how to apply God's laws to the diverse situations of life.

The second goal of Torah study is to know the Torah for its own sake, without practical applications. This goal is particularly relevant to the Written Torah. Even if we do not fully understand the words and intent, we still fulfill the mitzvah of Torah study when we read the Written Torah. As the Sages taught, "One should first learn superficially, and later analyze [the material] ... even if one does not [initially] understand what one has read" (*Avodah Zarah* 19a).

There is no value, however, in studying the Oral Torah if it is not understood properly. On the contrary, misreading the Oral Law will lead to errors in Halachic rulings and faulty conduct.

Attaining accurate insight into the practical application of Torah principles requires a breadth and depth of Torah scholarship. It is unreasonable to expect the entire people to reach such a level of erudition. For this reason, the practical side of Torah was transmitted orally. Only those who labor diligently in its study, receiving the traditions from the great scholars of the previous generation, will truly merit this knowledge. If this part of Torah had been committed to writing, many unlearned individuals would be falsely confident in rendering legal decisions, despite not having studied all of the relevant issues.

One might argue that perhaps the entire Torah should have been transmitted orally. But then Torah knowledge would be limited to only a select few. The Written Torah enables all to be exposed to Torah, on whatever level they are capable of comprehending.

Now we can better understand the Torah's account of Mount Sinai. When they first accepted the Oral Law, the people promised, "*Na'aseh.*" This aspect of Torah related to the entire people only in terms of its practical application – "We will do." It was with regard to the Written Torah, which is intellectually accessible to all, that the people added, "*VeNishma*" – "and we will understand."

❧ FIRST, "WE WILL DO"

It is natural to want to understand as much as possible and to act according to our understanding. The spiritual greatness of the Jewish people at Mount Sinai was their recognition of the benefit of not committing the Oral Law to writing so that their actions would best fulfill God's Will. This is the significance of their response "We will do": we accept upon ourselves to follow the practical teachings of the scholars and teachers of the Oral Law. Since this acceptance was equally relevant to all, regardless of intellectual capabilities, the verse emphasizes that "*the entire people* responded with a single voice."

After they had accepted upon themselves to observe the Torah according to the teachings of the rabbis, Moses then presented them with the Written Torah. We would have expected that the people would have shown particular love for the Written Law, since they could approach this Torah directly. But in an act of spiritual nobility, the Jewish people demonstrated their desire to first obey and observe the applied rulings of the Oral Law. Thus they announced: "We will do," and only afterward, "we will understand."

In summary: the Jewish people received two Torahs at Sinai. Moses first gave them the Oral Law, so they could fulfill the Torah's principle goal – proper conduct in this world. Then Moses transmitted the Written Law, enabling each individual to access Torah at his level, and preparing the people to receive the practical teachings of the Oral Law.

A Pure Revelation[1]

Moses awoke early in the morning and climbed Mount Sinai. (Ex. 34:4)

THE TEXT EMPHASIZES that Moses ascended the mountain at daybreak to receive the Torah. The Sages taught that Moses' subsequent descent from Sinai to transmit the Torah to the people also took place at first light. "Just as his ascent was at daybreak, so, too, his descent was at daybreak" (*Shabbat* 86a). Why is the hour of these events so significant?

❧ CRYSTAL CLEAR

The quality of Moses' prophecy was without equal. The Sages compared the unique clarity of his prophetic vision to an *aspaklariah me'irah*, a clear, transparent lens. This metaphor expresses the unique authenticity of the Divine revelation to Moses, to whom God spoke "face to face, in a vision and not in allegories" (Num. 12:8).

What made Moses' vision so uniquely accurate? His prophesy was true to its original Divine source; it was not influenced by societal needs or

---

1   Adapted from *Ein Ayah* vol. IV on *Shabbat* 86a (9:16).

political considerations. On the contrary, it is this pristine Divine revelation that dictates the proper path for society, the nation, and the entire world.

For this reason, the Torah stresses the hour of this historic event. Moses began his ascent to Sinai at first light – before the day's social interactions – thus indicating that the revelation at Sinai was independent of all social, political, and practical accommodations. It is precisely due to the Torah's absolute integrity that it has the power to vitiate life and renew creation, to refine humanity and uplift the world to the heights of purity and holiness.

◦ PRECISE TRANSMISSION

The Sages added an important corollary to this insight. It was not just Moses' original revelation that was free of worldly influences. The Torah's transmission to the people also retained its original authenticity. "Just as his ascent was at daybreak, so, too, his descent was at daybreak." The Torah's laws do not reflect the influence of social and political necessities. The Torah is the light of the Creator, the Divine Will giving life to the world, propelling the universe to advance in all aspects, material and spiritual.

The Torah that Moses brought down to the people of Israel was the exact same Torah that he received on Sinai – a complete Torah of absolute truth, transcending the limitations of our flawed world. "His descent was at daybreak," unaffected by the day's social interactions. The Torah remained pure, brought down to the world through the spiritual genius of the master prophet.

The Lesson of Mount Sinai[1]

W HAT DOES THE name "Sinai" mean? The Talmudic interpretation is surprising – even somewhat shocking:

What is Mount Sinai? The mountain that brought enmity (*sin'ah*)
upon the nations of the world." (*Shabbat* 89b)

What is the nature of this animosity? What does it have to do with
Mount Sinai?

ॐ WHY SINAI?

Where would one expect that God would reveal His Torah to the Jewish
people? The logical place would be on the holiest mountain in the world –
Jerusalem's Mount Moriah, the site of the Binding of Isaac, Jacob's holy "gate
to heaven" (Gen 28:17), the spot where both Temples once stood. Why did
the revelation of the Torah take place outside of the land of Israel, in the
middle of the desert?

The fact that the Torah was not given to the Jewish people in their own
land, but rather in a wilderness, in no-man's land, is very significant. This
indicates that the inner content of the Torah is relevant to all peoples. If

---

1 Adapted from *Ein Ayah* vol. IV on *Shabbat* 89b (9:121).

receiving the Torah required the special holiness of the Jewish people, then the Torah should have been given in a place that reflects that holiness. Revelation on Mount Sinai attests to the Torah's universal nature.

This idea is corroborated by the Talmudic tradition that "God offered the Torah to every nation and every tongue, but none accepted it until He came to Israel, who received it" (*Avodah Zarah* 2b). This Midrash is well-known, but it contains an implication that is often overlooked. How could God offer the nations something that is beyond their spiritual level? It is only because the Torah is relevant to all peoples that their refusal to accept it reflects so harshly on them.

The Torah's revelation on Mount Sinai, as a neutral location belonging to none and thus belonging to all, emphasizes the disappointment and estrangement from God that the nations brought upon themselves by rejecting the Torah and its ethical teachings. It is for this reason that Mount Sinai "brought enmity upon the nations of the world."

In the future, however, the nations will recognize this error and correct it:

> In those days, it will come to pass that ten men from all the languages of the nations will take hold of every Jew by the corner of his cloak and say, "Let us go with you, for we have heard that God is with you." (Zachariah 8:23)

Coercion at Sinai[1]

T HE TORAH DESCRIBES the remarkable events that preceded the Torah's revelation at Mount Sinai:

> Moses led the people out of the camp toward God and they stood at the bottom of the mountain. (Ex. 19:17)

The Midrash interprets the phrase "bottom of the mountain" quite literally: the people were standing, not at the foot of the mountain, but *underneath it.*

> The Holy One held the mountain over them like a bucket and warned them: If you accept the Torah – good. And if not – here you will be buried. (*Shabbat* 88a)

Would it not have been preferable for the Jewish people to accept the Torah willingly? Why does the Midrash teach that they were forced to accept it?

---

1   Adapted from *Ein Ayah* vol. IV on *Shabbat* 88a (9:67).

❧ LIMITS TO FREE WILL

It is essential that we have the ability to choose between right and wrong. It is through our free will that we develop spiritually and refine our ethical faculties. There are, however, limitations to our free will.

Not everything is subject to freedom of choice. Free will itself is an integral part of life and is beyond our control. We are not free to decide whether to choose or not. We must make an ethical choice. We decide what to choose, where to go, which path to take. But the necessity to choose, like life itself, is forced upon us.

If the Torah was simply a manual how to make good ethical decisions, it would be appropriate for Israel to be free to accept or reject the Torah. The Torah would belong to the realm of free will, and the fundamental decision whether to accept and follow the Torah would need to be made freely, without coercion.

But the Torah is much more than a moral guidebook. The Torah expresses our inner essence. When we violate the Torah's teachings, we become estranged from our own true selves. For this reason, the Torah needed to be given to Israel in a compulsory act, just as free will is an inherent aspect of our spiritual makeup and was imposed upon us without our consent.

❧ SUPPORTING THE WORLD

The corollary to this truth is that the Torah is not the private possession of the Jewish people. Within the inner realm of creation, all is interconnected and interrelated. The universe mandates the existence of the Torah and its acceptance by Israel.

Why did the Midrash use the image of an immense mountain dangling overhead as a metaphor for the inevitability of *Matan Torah*?

Mount Sinai merited a unique role on that decisive day. The mountain represented all of creation; it became the universe's center of gravity. Mount Sinai absorbed the quality of universality and was permeated with the force of inevitable destiny. It represented the impossibility of life, or any aspect of existence, without Israel accepting the Torah.

The Jewish people made their stand under the mountain. Like Atlas, they supported the entire universe – a universe that was concentrated within the mountain held over their heads. "If you accept the Torah, good" – for then you will have been faithful to your true essence, the truth of your very existence. "And if not, here you will be buried." The entire universe will rise up against you, just as you have rebelled against your true selves.

Connecting to Torah[1]

FOR RAV KOOK, it was axiomatic that the Jewish soul and the Torah are a match made in heaven. In his book analyzing the essential nature and value of Torah study, *Orot HaTorah*, he categorically asserted that *"The Torah is bound together with the spirit of Israel"* (12:1). This is true not only for the Jewish people as a whole, but also for each individual:

> Just as *Knesset Yisrael* [the national soul of Israel] can only realize its full potential in the land of Israel,[2] so, too, each individual Jew can only fulfill his spiritual potential through the Torah, which is the spiritual "land" suitable to the special qualities of the Jewish soul. All other studies are like foreign lands with regard to the spiritual development of Israel. (12:7)

While this is nice in theory, in practice things are not so simple. Not everyone takes to Torah study like a fish to water. If Torah study is indeed so natural to the Jewish soul, why do Jewish educators need to work so hard?

---

1   Adapted from *Orot HaTorah*, sections 2:1, 4:4, 4:5, 6:2, 7:1, 7:4, 9:1, 9:6, 9:8, 11:2, 12:1, 12:7.
2   Central national institutions of the Jewish people, such as the Temple, Sanhedrin, the monarchy, and prophecy, only exist in the land of Israel. See *Kuzari* 2:12, where medieval philosopher Rabbi Yehudah HaLevi uses a parable of a vineyard to explain this phenomenon. While a grapevine may grow in many lands, only in a certain climate and under particular soil conditions will the grapevine produce its fullest, choicest fruits.

Rav Kook was aware of this problem. There are a number of reasons why the words of Torah may not find a place in one's heart – some practical, some spiritual. In analyzing the reasons why a person may feel disconnected from Torah, Rav Kook noted several underlying causes.

⤴ APPRECIATING TORAH

To properly appreciate the value of Torah study, we must recognize the essential nature of the Torah. The Torah is a revelation of *ratzon Hashem*, God's Will in the world. It is only due to the limitations of our physical state that we are unable to recognize the Torah's true greatness.

Similarly, we need to have a proper appreciation for our Divine soul and its natural sense of morality. People occasionally err and stumble; but overall, we should have faith in our innate moral sensibilities. Thus there exists an inner correlation between the Torah's ethical teachings and the soul's inner qualities. The extent that one enjoys studying Torah is a function of refinement of character; the greater one's moral sensitivity, the more readily one will identify with the Torah and its teachings.

This fundamental insight is essential in order to properly appreciate Torah study. When Torah is studied in holiness, one may sense the greatness of the Torah and how it emanates from the very source of holiness.

⤴ ELEVATING THE DETAILS

A basic appreciation for Torah, however, is not enough. Even if one recognizes the Divine nature of the Torah, one may feel a sense of impatience when faced with its myriad laws and complex details. One may be attracted to lofty matters, and feel restricted and frustrated when studying the detailed minutiae of Halachah.

The remedy for these feelings of restriction is not to avoid Halachic studies but rather "*to elevate the significance of each detail of practical studies to the richness of its spiritual source*" (*Orot HaTorah* 9:8). A detail may acquire great significance when illuminated by a flash of insight or sudden inspiration. Success in "elevating the details" requires spiritual refinement and perseverance in the contemplative pursuit of the boundless heights of holiness.

In fact, each word of Torah contains infinite light, a reflection of the Torah's absolute morality. One who has learned to perceive this light will gain insight into the inner spiritual content of each detail.

FIND YOUR PORTION IN THE TORAH

An additional aspect that needs to be addressed is that not all areas of Torah appeal to all people equally. In general we should occupy ourselves with those pursuits that interest us. This is especially true regarding Torah study, as the Sages taught, "One only learns that which one's heart desires" (*Avodah Zarah* 19a).

Some have strayed from and even abandoned the Jewish people because they failed to follow their personal inclinations when choosing what area of Torah to study. They may have been predisposed to philosophical inquiry, but lacking appreciation for their own innate interests, they dedicated themselves to conventional Halachic studies. Unsurprisingly, they felt an inner resistance to this course of study, since it was not compatible to their natural inclinations. Had they focused on learning more suitable topics, they would have realized that their inner opposition to Halachic studies was not due to some flaw in this important area of knowledge, but because their soul demanded a different field of Torah study.

Since they failed to understand the root cause of their inner conflict with Torah study, they attempted to suppress their natural tendencies. But as soon as an alternative path became available, they rejected the Torah and the faith of Israel. Some of these individuals subsequently attempted to promote great ideals lacking practical foundations, and they misled the world with their false visions.

Others are naturally drawn to the sciences and secular studies. These individuals should follow their natural interests, while setting aside set times for Torah study. Then they will succeed in both areas. As the Sages counseled in *Pirkei Avot* 2:2, "It is good to combine the study of Torah with worldly endeavors."

TISHA BE'AV
תשעה באב

The Beit HaMikdash – Beyond Our Imagination

After the great destruction that befell us, after our beloved House was burnt down and the honor of our lives was lost, after our bones were scattered at the entrance of Sheol, after the voice of our inner life, strong and courageous with the power of Divine might and eternity, was laid low and silenced – it became impossible for us to even imagine the nobility and the power, the beauty and the purity . . . of the holy Temple service.

(*Olat Re'iyah* vol. 1, pp. 117–118)

꙲

The Wall of Iron[1]

T HE *BEIT HAMIKDASH*, the holy Temple in Jerusalem, was a focal point of Divine service, prayer, and prophecy; a vehicle to bring the *Shechinah* into the world. The current state of the world, without the *Beit HaMikdash*, is one of estrangement from God. When the Temple was destroyed, the Talmud teaches, the gates of prayer were locked and a wall of iron separates us from our Heavenly Father (*Berachot* 32b).

Why did the Sages describe this breach of communication with God as a "wall of iron"? Why not, for example, a "wall of stone"?

꙳ A WORLD RULED BY IRON

The metaphor of an iron wall, Rav Kook explained, is precise for several reasons. A stone wall is built slowly, stone by stone, layer by layer. An iron wall is more complex to construct; but when it is erected, it is set up quickly. The Temple's destruction and the resultant estrangement from God was not a gradual process, but a sudden calamity for the Jewish people and the entire world, like an iron gate swinging shut.

But there is a deeper significance to this barrier of iron. The fundamental aim of the Temple is the exact opposite of iron. Iron is a symbol of death

---

1 Adapted from *Ein Ayah* vol. I on *Berachot* 32b (5:76).

and destruction; implements of war and slaughter are fashioned from metal and iron. Iron is a material used to shorten life. The Temple, on the other hand, is meant to lengthen life. Its purpose is to promote universal peace and enlightenment – "My House will be called a house of prayer for all the nations" (Isaiah 56:7). The incompatibility between iron and the Temple is so great that iron could not be used to hew the stones used in building the Temple (Deut. 27:5, *Middot* 3:4).

With the Temple's destruction, the sweet music of prayer and song was replaced by the jarring cacophony of iron and steel, reaping destruction and cutting down life. At that tragic time, the spiritual and prophetic influence of the Temple was supplanted by the rule of iron. Only when justice and integrity will be restored, when the world will recognize the principles of morality and truth, will this wall of iron come down, and the *Beit HaMikdash* will once again take its place as a world center of prayer and holy inspiration.

※

Rebuilding the World with Love[1]

   ❧   RECTIFYING BASELESS HATRED

Why was the Second Temple destroyed? The Sages in *Yoma* 9b noted that the people at that time studied Torah, observed mitzvot, and performed good deeds. Their great failure was in *sinat chinam* – baseless hatred. It was internal strife and conflict that ultimately brought about the Temple's destruction.

How may we rectify this sin of *sinat chinam*? Rav Kook wrote, in one of his most oft-quoted statements:

> If we were destroyed, and the world with us, due to baseless hatred, then we shall rebuild ourselves, and the world with us, with baseless love [*ahavat chinam*]. (*Orot HaKodesh* vol. III, p. 324)

This call for baseless love could be interpreted as following Maimonides' advice on how to correct bad character traits. In the fourth chapter of *Shemonah Perakim*, Maimonides taught that negative traits are corrected by temporarily overcompensating and practicing the opposite extreme. For

---

1   Adapted from *Orot HaKodesh* vol. III, pp. 324–334; *Malachim K'vnei Adam*, pp. 262, 483–485.

example, one who is naturally stingy should balance this trait by acting overly generous, until he succeeds in uprooting his miserliness. Similarly, by going to the extreme of *ahavat chinam*, we repair the trait of *sinat chinam*.

This interpretation, however, is not Rav Kook's line of thought. *Ahavat chinam* is not a temporary remedy, but an ideal, the result of our perception of the world's underlying unity and goodness.

THE SOURCE OF HATRED

Why do we hate others? We may think of many reasons why, but these explanations are not the real source for our hatred of other people. They are merely signs and indications of our hatred. It is a lack of clarity of thought that misleads us into believing that these are the true causes of hatred.

The true source of hate comes from our *otzar hachaim*, our inner resource of life. This fundamental life-force pushes us to live and thrive, and opposes all that it views as different and threatening. Ultimately, our hate is rooted in *sinat chinam* – groundless and irrational animosity, just because something is different.

Yet even in hatred lies a hidden measure of love. Baseless love and baseless hatred share a common source, a love of life and the world. This common source hates that which is evil and destructive, and loves that which is good and productive.

How can we overcome our hatred? If we can uncover the depth of good in what we perceive as negative, we will be able to see how good will result even from actions and ideas that we oppose. We will then recognize that our reasons for hatred are unfounded, and transform our hatred into love and appreciation.

"I BURN WITH LOVE"

This idea of *ahavat chinam* was not just a theoretical concept. Rav Kook was well-known for his profound love for all Jews, even those far removed from Torah and mitzvot. When questioned why he loved Jews distant from the ideals of Torah, he would respond, "Better I should err on the side of baseless love, than I should err on the side of baseless hatred."

Stories abound of Rav Kook's extraordinary love for other Jews, even those intensely antagonistic to his ways and beliefs. Once Rav Kook was publicly humiliated by a group of extremists who showered him with waste water in the streets of Jerusalem. The entire city was in an uproar over this scandalous act. The legal counsel of the British Mandate advised Rav Kook to press charges against the hooligans, promising that they would be promptly deported from the country. The legal counsel, however, was astounded by the Chief Rabbi's response.

> I have no interest in court cases. Despite what they did to me, I love them. I am ready to kiss them, so great is my love! I burn with love for every Jew.

ஃ PRACTICAL STEPS TOWARD *AHAVAT CHINAM*

In his magnum opus *Orot HaKodesh*, Rav Kook gave practical advice on how to achieve this love.

- Love for the Jewish people does not start from the heart, but from the head. To truly love and understand the Jewish people – each individual Jew and the nation as a whole – requires a wisdom that is both insightful and multifaceted. This intellectual inquiry is an important discipline of Torah study.

- Loving others does not mean indifference to baseness and moral decline. Our goal is to awaken knowledge and morality, integrity, and refinement; to clearly mark the purpose of life, its purity and holiness. Even our acts of loving-kindness should be based on a hidden *Gevurah*, an inner outrage at the world's – and thus our own – spiritual failures.

- If we take note of others' positive traits, we will come to love them with an inner affection. This is not a form of insincere flattery, nor does it mean white-washing their faults and foibles. But by concentrating on their positive characteristics – and every person has a good side – the negative aspects become less significant.

- This method provides an additional benefit. The Sages cautioned against joining with the wicked and exposing oneself to their negative influence. But if we connect to their positive traits, then this contact will not endanger our own moral and spiritual purity.

- We can attain a high level of love for Israel by deepening our awareness of the inner ties that bind together all the souls of the Jewish people, throughout all the generations. In the following revealing passage, Rav Kook expressed his own profound sense of connection with and love for every Jewish soul:

> Listen to me, my people! I speak to you from my soul, from within my innermost soul. I call out to you from the living connection by which I am bound to all of you, and by which all of you are bound to me. I feel this more deeply than any other feeling: that only you – all of you, all of your souls, throughout all of your generations – you alone are the meaning of my life. In you I live. In the aggregation of all of you, my life has that content that is called 'life.' Without you, I have nothing. All hopes, all aspirations, all purpose in life, all that I find inside myself – these are only when I am with you. I need to connect with all of your souls. I must love you with a boundless love. . . .
>
> Each one of you, each individual soul from the aggregation of all of you, is a great spark from the torch of infinite light, which enlightens my existence. You give meaning to life and work, to Torah and prayer, to song and hope. It is through the conduit of your being that I sense everything and love everything. (*Shemonah Kevatzim*, vol. I, sec. 163)

The Beauty of the Universe[1]

EVERY DAY WE pray for the restoration of the *Beit HaMikdash*. Why is this spiritual center so important for us?

The Sages noted that the words *dei'ah* (knowledge) and *Mikdash* (Temple) both appear in verses 'sandwiched' between God's Name (I Sam. 2:3 and Ex. 15:17). Is there a special connection between the two?

> Rabbi Elazar said: Whenever a person has *dei'ah*, it is as if the Temple has been built in his days. (*Berachot* 33a)

What exactly did Rabbi Elazar mean by "a person with *dei'ah*"? And what does this quality of wisdom have to do with rebuilding the *Beit HaMikdash*?

❧ TRUE *DA'AT*

We must first understand the concept of *dei'ah*. Having *dei'ah* means much more than just being knowledgeable. People who lack *dei'ah* approach matters only using their powers of logic and reasoning. They fail to recognize that the intellect is but one faculty of the human soul. In addition to intellectual abilities, we have character traits, emotions, and powers of imagination.

---

1 Adapted from *Ein Ayah* vol. I on *Berachot* 33a (5:96).

True *da'at* is knowing how to utilize all the faculties of the soul. Spiritual perfection can only be attained through a holistic approach that engages all aspects of the soul and all pathways of faith.

ᴥ THE BEAUTY OF THE UNIVERSE

But what does this have to do with the *Beit HaMikdash*? The Sages used an intriguing expression to describe the Temple: "the Beauty of the universe" (*Zevachim* 54b). Why did they single out "beauty" as the Temple's primary characteristic? This statement is significant, for it indicates the central function of the *Beit HaMikdash* – to engage our sense of beauty and elevate our imaginative powers.[2] The imagination is a powerful resource, and the Temple's aesthetic qualities served to promote the world's spiritual advance through this faculty of the soul. When the *Beit HaMikdash* stood in Jerusalem, it had a profound influence on the imagination, as it projected images of sublime purity and holy splendor. This impact on the imagination then inspired and elevated the character traits and conduct of those visiting its courtyards.

We may distinguish between two different aspects of the Temple's influence. The first is in terms of the Temple's intrinsic holiness and the impact of this holiness on those observing the Temple service. The second aspect is in terms of the receptivity of the human soul. God gave us powers of imagination so that we will be receptive to the Temple's splendor and holiness. These two aspects of the Temple's influence correspond to the two Names of God, placed before and after the word *Mikdash*.

ᴥ ELEVATING THE IMAGINATION

Now we may understand Rabbi Elazar's statement. Individuals who are blessed with *dei'ah* –who are wise enough to value all faculties of the

2   The ultimate purpose of the Temple is to attain *Hashra'at Shechinah*, the indwelling of God's Presence in Israel, as it says (Ex. 25:8), "They shall make Me a Sanctuary and I will dwell among them." Rav Kook understood that this goal indicates the Temple's function as a center of prophecy and *ruach hakodesh* (see Jer. Talmud *Sukkah* 5a), and this requires the elevation of the imaginative powers, an essential faculty for prophecy and holy inspiration.

soul, including their imaginative powers – it is as if the *Beit HaMikdash* was rebuilt in their days. With their wisdom, they are able to recreate for themselves and their immediate circle a small measure of the Temple's holy influence. They recognize that their powers of imagination were created for a sacred purpose. While in terms of cold logic, the imagination may appear to be of little value, God placed it in the human soul for its potential to promote spiritual growth. Those crowned with *dei'ah* are able to utilize and elevate all of their faculties in genuine holiness.

Rav Kook likened the Temple's enlightening influence on the soul to the first rays of morning sunlight, as they provide warmth and nourishment:

> The sublime beauty, the Divine splendor, attracts and draws the soul to itself. It awakens the soul from its sleep and rejuvenates all of its powers. It shines over the soul like sunlight over a cherished plant, cultivating all of its aspects, full of strength and beauty, pleasantness and vitality.
>
> Our yearnings to be connected to the Temple – to God's House on the mountain summit, to the service of the *kohanim*, the song of the Levites, and the *ma'amad* (deputation) of the Israelites, to share all of the nation's soul-ties to its holy abode – these yearnings awaken the "beauty of the universe" in the hearts of Israel each day. They establish an elevated Temple inside the soul of each individual, as we begin the day by reciting the order of offerings and incense in our morning prayers.
>
> (*Shemonah Kevatzim* vol. I, sec. 606)

The Call for Holy Splendor[1]

LIKE A GRIEVING lion, God roars each day:

> Woe to My children! On account of their sins I have destroyed My House, set fire to My sanctuary, and exiled them among the nations! (*Berachot* 3a)

If the Sages are correct, and God is so deeply distraught about the destruction of the *Beit HaMikdash* – then why does He not rebuild it?

EMULATING GOD

Before answering this question, we must first examine a more basic issue: how does one go about living a life of holiness? The path to holiness, Rav Kook explained, is based on a single fundamental rule: *emulating God*. We should strive to compare and equate our conduct to God's elevated ways. This was King David's guiding principle: "I have placed God before me at all times" (Ps. 16:8). The phrase "I have placed" (שִׁוִּיתִי) may be translated as "I have equated" – "I have equated God to myself at all times."

The Torah articulates this idea with the command, "You shall follow in His ways" (Deut. 28:9). As the Sages explained, "Just as God is gracious and compassionate, so you should be gracious and compassionate" (*Shabbat*

---

1 Adapted from *Orot HaKodesh* vol. III, pp. 199–200.

133b). Ethical conduct, positive character traits, and, in fact, all mitzvot and good deeds – they are all based on this principle of emulating God.

But is it possible for the finite to emulate the Infinite? The Sages spoke of "likening the created form to its Creator" (*Breishit Rabbah* 24:1). Such comparisons require our imaginative faculties. The Hebrew word *dimayon* means both "comparison" and "imagination." It is only through our powers of imagination that we are able to envision the application of Divine traits in our lives. From here it is clear that the imagination is a fundamental tool in serving God. And as one advances in holiness, one's imagination is strengthened and purified.

The various manifestations of a life of holiness – whether a heightened sensitivity to the feelings and property of others, or aesthetic embellishments when performing mitzvot (*hiddur mitzvah*) – are all expressions of serving God through one's imaginative powers. Such conduct reflects the refinement of one's soul and the richness of one's imagination.

❧ THE NATION'S POWERS OF IMAGINATION

The same principle holds true for the nation as a whole. The awe-inspiring splendor of the *Beit HaMikdash*, the majestic nobility of the priestly garments, the sanctity and purity of the Temple service – all of these presuppose the importance of a strong and robust imagination. The Sages referred to the *Beit HaMikdash* as "the Beauty of the universe" to highlight the Temple's primary function in engaging the aesthetic and imaginative faculties.

Our imaginative powers fulfill their ultimate purpose when they serve as an instrument for enlightenment. In its highest levels, this enlightenment manifests itself as prophetic inspiration and, on the collective level, God's Divine Presence in Israel.

However, proper use of the imagination requires mental and practical preparation. One cannot attain a richness of God-directed imagination while suffering from ignorance and unrefined character traits. Only wise and virtuous individuals, Maimonides asserted, can attain prophecy (Fundamentals of Torah 7:1). And on the national level, only when the

Jewish collective has attained an appropriate ethical and spiritual level will it be possible to restore the *Beit HaMikdash*. The focal point of Divine beauty in the world requires prerequisite levels of both cognitive and practical holiness.

But while the nation may not be ready for the actual rebuilding of the *Beit HaMikdash*, we still feel the soul's demand for this lofty spiritual splendor. The soul cries out for its powers of imagination to be cleansed and elevated, purified and enriched. These cries of anguish, this profound sense of loss, may be heard in the terrible roars of Divine grief: "I have destroyed My House, set fire to My sanctuary, and exiled My children among the nations!"

The Three Watches of the Night[1]

ANGUISHED ROARS

All over the world there are flourishing Jewish communities, blessed with thriving synagogues, bustling schools, and prominent *yeshivot*. But with all of this Torah study and mitzvah-observance, do we feel the absence of the *Beit HaMikdash*? Are we aware of our state of exile and dispersion?

The anguished roars of a lion – that is how the prophet describes God's constant grief over the loss of the Holy Temple. "God roars from on high; He calls out from His holy dwelling, roaring over His habitation" (Jeremiah 25:30).

The Sages were able to hear these roars and translate them for us: "Woe to My children! On account of their sins, I have destroyed My House and set fire to My sanctuary and exiled them among the nations of the world" (*Berachot* 3a).

THREE WATCHES

The Rabbis also knew at what hour these heavenly cries may be heard. These roars, they taught, take place during the three watches of the night.

---

1   Adapted from *Ein Ayah* vol. I on *Berachot* 3a (1:6).

(The darkness of night is a common metaphor for the exile.) And there are even signs that indicate the exact time of these anguished cries:

> The night consists of three watches, and during each watch the Holy One sits and roars like a lion. . . . The sign for this: in the first watch, a donkey brays; in the second, dogs howl; and in the third, a baby nurses from its mother and a woman converses with her husband.

What is the meaning of these strange signs – donkeys braying, dogs howling, babies nursing, and early-morning conversations?

THE FLAWED SERVICE OF ISRAEL IN EXILE

We must first understand the significance of these night watches. The watches are a metaphor for underlying spiritual mechanisms in the universe. Each watch corresponds to the elevation of higher realms, an elevation that is a result of Israel's service of God in this world. Since the Temple's destruction and the exile of Israel, however, the Jewish nation has been reduced to an atrophied spiritual life. This decline has diminished the overall level of Divine providence in the world. The roars of heavenly anguish during the night watches are an expression of the cosmic pain caused by this spiritual decline.

Why are there *three* watches? The three watches correspond to the three basic levels in which we serve God: (1) through our actions, (2) by refining our character traits, and (3) by deepening our understanding and knowledge. Sadly, all three aspects have been adversely affected by the exile and the absence of the *Beit HaMikdash*.

DEEDS AND TRAITS

The first form of serving God is through deeds and actions. When the Jewish people are on an elevated spiritual plane, their mitzvot and acts of kindness are guided by a profound awareness of God's presence. Due to the detrimental influences of exile, however, all of our actions are tainted by an overall atmosphere of self-centeredness and materialism. This causes our service of God to lose its reparative quality of *tikkun*. Lacking the guidance of

Divine wisdom, materialistic tendencies are reinforced. This phenomenon is particularly apparent regarding mitzvot that involve physical pleasures, such as the mitzvah to rejoice on the holidays.

For this reason, the sign of the first watch is the braying of a donkey (in Hebrew, *chamor*), indicating the awakening of materialistic tendencies (*chomriut*). This is a basic aspect of human nature – "For man is born a wild donkey" (Job 11:12) – that is bolstered by the negative influences of exile and its limited spiritual life.

The second night-watch corresponds to our service of God through the acquisition of positive character traits, such as kindness, generosity, and humility. The current state of the world, however, with its lack of holy influences, fosters various negative traits. This is not due to the body's physicality but rather because we lack an accurate image of pure and refined traits, as we are unable to faithfully model ourselves after God's traits of kindness and compassion.

The sign for the distortion of this service is the howling of dogs. Dogs symbolize negative traits, especially insolence (see Isaiah 56:11). Greed and brazenness are the source for many other flawed traits.

✿ SERVICE OF THE INTELLECT

The final watch corresponds to the highest form of serving God – using our cognitive powers. There are two levels in this *avodah*: those who study Halachah and the revealed parts of Torah, and those who delve into deeper esoteric studies. Unlike the service of God in actions and character traits, Torah learning cannot be debased. As the Sages taught, "Words of Torah cannot contract ritual impurity" (*Berachot* 22a). Therefore the signs of the third watch are positive ones, signs of Divine intimacy and beneficence – a baby nursing and a wife conversing with her husband.

However, even this level is detrimentally influenced by the exile. What is the heavenly sign for those who study the revealed parts of Torah? "A baby nursing from its mother." This indicates a state that is incomplete, an intellectual service not fully developed; it is therefore symbolized by a nursing baby.

Those who study on a deeper level, contemplating the nature of God with philosophical and mystical inquiries, are blessed with a revealed love of God. The sign for this level is one of love and affection – "a woman conversing with her husband." Nonetheless, even this holy service appears to be deficient, as the Sages described it as a "conversation" (*mesaperet*), the relating of stories without deeper and truer content. Once again, this state is due to our current lack of Divine inspiration and prophetic wisdom.

Anticipating Redemption[1]

THERE ARE SIX measures, the Sages taught, by which we are judged:

> When brought for heavenly judgment, one is questioned: "Were your business dealings honest? Did you set fixed hours for Torah study? Did you engage in procreation? Did you anticipate redemption? Did you discuss wisdom? Did you discern new insights?" (*Shabbat* 31a)

Most of these questions indeed are the cornerstones of a life well-lived. But the fourth one – "*Did you anticipate redemption?*" – why is that so important? Don't we all hope for the best? What does this trait reveal about how one has lived one's life?

✑ PART OF THE NATION

It is important to understand that this anticipation is not simply hoping that our personal difficulties will quickly be resolved. Rather, it means that we should anticipate the redemption of Israel and all of humanity. As Rashi explains, one should look forward to the fulfillment of the visions of the prophets.

This demand is not a trivial one. As individuals we are easily caught up

---

1   Adapted from *Olat Re'iyah* vol. I, pp. 279–280; *Ein Ayah* vol. III on *Shabbat* 31a (2:164).

with our own personal problems and issues. In truth, we should feel that we are like a limb of a great organism. We should recognize that we are part of a nation, which, in turn, is part of all humanity. The betterment of each individual contributes to the life of the larger community, thus advancing the redemption of the nation and the universe.

The question "*Tzapita leyeshu'ah?*" is an important measure of one's life. It is the yardstick that determines whether our lives have acquired a selfless, universal quality. By anticipating the redemption of the greater community, we demonstrate that we were able to raise ourselves above the narrow concerns of our private lives. We strive not just for personal ambitions, but also for the ultimate elevation of the nation and the entire world. We are part of the nation; its joys are our joys and its redemption is our redemption.

৯ THE SENTRY

It is instructive to note that the heavenly tribunal does not ask about our hopes (*tikvah*) for redemption, but rather our anticipation (*tzipiyah*) of redemption. The word *tzipiyah* indicates a constant watchfulness, like a soldier posted to the lookout (*tatzpit*), serving at his observation post for days and even years. The sentry may not abandon his watch, even though he observes no changes.

We, too, are on the lookout. We should examine every incident that occurs in the world. With each new development, we should consider whether this is perhaps something that will advance the redemption of Israel and the entire world.

However, *tzipiyah leyeshu'ah* is not merely passive observation. Woe to the army whose sentries perceive a threat but fail to take action. The moment there is some development in the field, the soldiers must respond swiftly, to defend or retreat. Our *tzipiyah* also includes the readiness to act promptly. While these two traits – constant watchfulness and rapid response – may appear contradictory, they are both included in the obligation of *tzipiyah leyeshu'ah*.

The Poel Mizrachi Kitchen[1]

THINGS WERE NOT looking good for Avraham Mavrach. It was already the first of the month of Av, and the secretary would not let him present his urgent question to the Chief Rabbinate. The rabbis were in an important meeting, the secretary explained, and could not be disturbed.

❧ THE KOSHER KITCHEN

Mr. Avraham Mavrach was a founding member of the Poel Mizrachi, established in 1922 for religious pioneers in *Eretz Yisrael*. One of the most important decisions made during the first assembly of the Poel Mizrachi was to open kosher kitchens for new immigrants and workers. This was necessary since the religious workers could not eat in the Histadrut kitchens, where non-kosher food was served and the Sabbath was desecrated.

As Avraham later described in the *Hatzofeh* newspaper:

> The religious pioneers suffered greatly. They could not afford to eat in a restaurant and enjoy a hot meal, and on Shabbat they missed the Jewish milieu and an atmosphere of holiness. Therefore we established the kitchens of the Poel Mizrachi to provide the religious workers with

---

1 Adapted from *Mo'adei HaRe'iyah*, pp. 539–543.

inexpensive and tasty meals, and also to serve as a social center. The workers would read, hold meetings, discuss, attend classes and lectures. They organized Torah classes in the evenings, and they would dance on joyous occasions. The kitchens were filled with singing; especially on Shabbat and the holidays, they sang the *zemirot* with holy yearnings and great emotion. It is not surprising that these kosher kitchens also attracted many non-religious workers.

Although the food was sold at cost, not all of the diners could afford to eat everything on the limited menu. However, the meat portions and soups were a necessary staple for the hungry manual laborers.

✥ THE PROBLEM OF THE NINE DAYS

It was regarding these meat meals that a serious problem arose. During the Nine Days of Av, eating meat is prohibited due to national mourning over the destruction of the Temple. The administrators of the Jerusalem branch of the Poel Mizrachi met to find an alternative for the meat meals, especially for the manual laborers. Unfortunately, they were unable to think of an appropriate substitute. Some of them despaired. "Why should we assume responsibility for this?" Lacking a better alternative, they wanted to close down the kitchen for the duration of the Nine Days.

One member, however, refused to give up – Avraham Mavrach. He suggested turning to the Chief Rabbinate; perhaps the rabbis would find a leniency that would permit the new customers to eat meat so that they would not go back to eating in the non-kosher kitchens. The other members laughed at this suggestion. "Do you really think that the Rabbinate will agree to the slaughter of sheep and oxen during the Nine Days in the holy city of Jerusalem?"

In fact, no one was even willing to accompany Avraham to the Chief Rabbinate. So, on the first of Av, he went alone. The Rabbinate secretary, however, refused to let him interrupt the meeting in order to speak with the rabbis.

"But it is an urgent question," Avraham explained. "I come as a representative of the Poel Mizrachi." At Avraham's insistence, Rabbi Samuel Weber, chief secretary of the Rabbinate, came out of the meeting and listened to the problem. Rabbi Weber suggested arranging for the completion of a Talmudic tractate every day, and then serving meat at the *se'udat mitzvah* (a meal celebrating the fulfillment of a mitzvah). Avraham responded that such an arrangement would be nearly impossible to implement.

Rabbi Weber then disappeared into the Rabbinate chambers. After a few minutes, he beckoned Avraham to follow.

✎ RAV KOOK'S DECISION

As he entered, Avraham saw Rav Kook at the head of the table, with Rabbi Yaakov Meir to his right and other prominent rabbis seated around the table. Rav Kook asked Avraham to approach the table. Avraham stood before the rabbis and explained the purpose of the kitchen, describing the great benefit it provided to the members of the Poel Mizrachi and the workers who remained faithful to their heritage.

"I am aware of the importance of the kitchen," Rav Kook responded. He then sank into deep thought. The other rabbis waited in silence for Rav Kook's decision.

Rav Kook turned to Avraham. "Do you think that some of the workers who eat there will end up going to a non-kosher kitchen?"

"Yes," Avraham responded. "They ate there beforehand."

"If that is the case," Rav Kook pronounced, "your kitchen is serving a *se'udat mitzvah*. 'Let the humble eat and be satisfied' (Ps. 27:22)."

Astounded, Avraham remained frozen to his spot. Rav Kook smiled. "Do you have another question?" Avraham replied that he was uncertain about the Rav's decision. Did this mean that *everyone* could eat meat there? Rav Kook repeated his words, and explained that everyone – even those who would not be tempted to eat at a non-kosher kitchen – could eat meat in the kitchen because it would be serving a *se'udat mitzvah*. Despite his amazement, Avraham managed to steal a glance at the other rabbis in the room. It seemed that they, too, were surprised by the Rav's decision, but they raised no objections.

❧ SE'UDAT MITZVAH FOR ALL

Rabbi Zvi Kaplan wrote an article analyzing this unusual Halachic decision at length. For those workers who would have eaten in the non-kosher kitchen, it is clearly preferable that they disregard the custom of not eating meat during the Nine Days rather than violate the Biblical prohibition against eating non-kosher food. But how could Rav Kook permit meat to those who would not have eaten non-kosher food?

Rabbi Kaplan noted that at a *se'udat mitzvah* during the Nine Days, permission to eat meat is granted not only for those performing the mitzvah (such as a *brit milah* or completing a tractate of Talmud), but for all who are present. Every Jew is responsible to make sure another Jew eats kosher food. A meal that accomplishes this goal certainly qualifies as a *se'udat mitzvah*. The simple meals provided by the Poel Mizrachi kitchen in those years saved many Jews from eating non-kosher meals. Rav Kook therefore was able to permit all present to eat, since, as he explained, "your kitchen is serving a *se'udat mitzvah*."

Bibliography

Ein Ayah – commentary on Talmudic Midrashim, arranged according to the book *Ein Ya'akov*.[1] Rav Kook began writing on tractate *Berachot* while serving as rabbi in Zaumel. He wanted to publish *Ein Ayah* while in Jaffa in 1906, but lacked sufficient funds for the undertaking. He continued to add material over the years, penning his final entry (two-thirds the way through tractate *Shabbat*) in Jerusalem in 1934 (he passed away the following year). As in his other early work, *Midbar Shur*, this commentary reflected his fervent belief that our generation must deepen its understanding of the Torah's underlying philosophical principles. Published by HaMachon al shem HaRav Tzvi Yehudah Kook (Jerusalem: 1995).

Igrot HaRe'iyah – three-volume collection of letters penned by Rav Kook between the years 1886 and 1919. Published by Mossad HaRav Kook, Jerusalem, 1962. A fourth volume for the years 1920 through 1925 was published by HaMachon al shem HaRav Tzvi Yehudah Kook (Jerusalem: 1984).

---

1   A compilation of Aggadic material from the Talmud by Rabbi Jacob ben Solomon ibn Habib, first published in 1516.

Ma'amarei HaRe'iyah – two volumes of articles and lectures, many originally published in various periodicals, collected by Rabbis Elisha Aviner and David Landau. Published by Mossad HaRav Kook (Jerusalem: 1984).

Midbar Shur – sermons written by Rav Kook while serving as rabbi in Zaumel and Boisk from 1894 to 1896. One of Rav Kook's first writings, but mysteriously lost. Finally published by HaMachon al shem HaRav Tzvi Yehudah Kook (Jerusalem: 1999).

Mo'adei HaRe'iyah – a blend of stories and writings of Rav Kook about the holidays by Rabbi Moshe Tzvi Neriah. Published by Moriah (Jerusalem: 1982).

Olat Re'iyah – two-volume commentary on the prayer book. Rav Kook began this project while in London during WWI, and continued after his return to Jerusalem. However, he only wrote as far as midway through the introductory psalms (*Pesukei deZimra*) of the morning prayers. Rabbi Tzvi Yehudah Kook completed the work by collecting relevant texts from various unpublished writings, and published it in 1939, several years after his father's death. Published by Mossad HaRav Kook (Jerusalem: 1983).

Orot – collection of essays, many analyzing Israel's national rebirth. The book was arranged by Rabbi Tzvi Yehudah Kook and first published in 1920. Despite rabbinical controversy concerning certain passages in the book, Rabbi Tzvi Yehudah taught that this work is, in comparison to Rav Kook's other writings, his "Holy of Holies." Published by Mossad HaRav Kook (Jerusalem: 1982).

Orot HaKodesh – expositions on Divine service, prophecy, the spiritual experience, ethics, etc., collected and organized from Rav Kook's diaries (*Shemonah Kevatzim*) by his student, Rabbi David Cohen (known as "the Nazir"). The Nazir spent twelve years preparing the four-volume work, considered by many to be Rav Kook's magnum opus. Published by Mossad HaRav Kook (Jerusalem: 1985).

Orot HaTeshuvah – on the repentance of the individual, the nation, and the universe, first published in Jerusalem in 1925. Rav Kook wrote the first three chapters, while the rest were collected from his writings and organized by Rabbi Tzvi Yehudah Kook. Rav Kook emphasized the importance of studying this book; he, himself, would review it during the month of Elul as a spiritual preparation for the High Holidays. Published in Jerusalem, 1977.

Orot HaTorah – short work on the metaphysical "importance of Torah, its study, and practical guidance" (from the cover page). Rabbi Tzvi Yehudah Kook collected these writings on the subject of Torah five years after his father's passing, in order to create a work similar to *Orot HaTeshuvah*. Published by Choshen (Jerusalem: 1973).

Rosh Milin – mystical reflections on the Hebrew alphabet and vowels. Rav Kook composed this short treatise while in London during World War I. It is considered to be one of Rav Kook's most difficult and esoteric works. Published by Yeshivat HaChaim veHaShalom (Jerusalem: 1972).

Glossary of Hebrew Terms

Ahavat Hashem – love for God

Amidah – the central prayer recited quietly while standing (*lit.* "standing")

Arba'ah Minim – the four species used in Succoth holiday rituals

Avodah – service (*usu.* of God)

Avot – the Patriarchs Abraham, Isaac and Jacob

Beit HaMikdash – the Holy Temple in Jerusalem

Brachah (*pl. Brachot*) – blessings

Chametz – leavened foods forbidden during the Passover holiday

Eretz Yisrael – the land of Israel

Etrog – citron fruit, one of the four species used in Succoth holiday rituals

Halachah – Jewish law

Haggadah – text that sets out the order of the Passover Seder

Hetter Mechirah – legal permit to allow farming during the Sabbatical year by selling land to a non-Jew

Kavannah – intent or mental preparation for prayer

Kehunah – priesthood

Ketoret – incense offered in the Temple

Klal – the community or nation

Kohen (*pl. kohanim*) – a priest, descended from Aaron

Maror – bitter herbs eaten at the Passover Seder

Mashiach – king of Davidic lineage who will rule during the Messianic Era

Matan Torah – the revelation of the Torah at Mount Sinai

Matzah – unleavened bread eaten on Passover to commemorate the hasty Exodus from Egypt

Mitzvah (pl. Mitzvot) – one of the 613 commandments of the Torah

Mehadrin – highest or strictest level of Halachic observance

Mikdash – the holy Temple in Jerusalem

Muktzeh – items that may not be handled on the Sabbath and holidays

Musaf – the additional prayer recited on the Sabbath and holidays

Neshamah – the soul

Segulah – something's inner essence or intrinsic quality (*lit.* "a treasure")

Shabbat – the Sabbath

Shechinah – God's Presence in the world

Shofar – the ram's horn blown on Rosh Hashanah

Sukkah – a thatched hut used as a temporary dwelling during the Succoth holiday

Tefillah – prayer

Terumah – a tithe on produce grown in the land of Israel, given to the *kohanim*

Teshuvah – repentance (*lit.* "return")

Tikun – correction, repair

Tzaddik (pl. Tzaddikim) – a righteous person

Yeshivah (pl. Yeshivot) – a higher institute of Torah study

Yom Ha'Atzmaut – Israel Independence Day

Index

Rabbi ABRAHAM ISAAC KOOK (1865–1935), the celebrated first Chief Rabbi of pre-state Israel, is recognized as being among the most important Jewish thinkers of all times. His writings reflect the mystic's search for underlying unity in all aspects of life and the world, and his unique personality similarly united a rare combination of talents and gifts. Rav Kook was a prominent rabbinical authority and active public leader, but at the same time, a deeply religious mystic. He was both Talmudic scholar and poet, original thinker and saintly tzaddik.

After graduating with a B.A. in mathematics from Yeshiva University (New York), Rabbi CHANAN MORRISON studied for several years at Yeshivat Mercaz HaRav, the Jerusalem yeshiva founded by Rav Kook in 1924. He was ordained after completing rabbinical studies in the Ohr Torah Stone (Efrat) and Midrash Sephardi (Jerusalem) rabbinical seminaries.

Rabbi Morrison taught Jewish studies for several years in Harrisburg, PA, before returning to Israel. He and his family subsequently settled in Mitzpe Yericho, an Israeli community in the Judean Desert. In an effort to maintain contact with former students, Rabbi Morrison began emailing articles on the weekly Torah portion based on Rav Kook's writings. Over the years, this email list grew quickly and now reaches thousands of readers from all over the world.

Rabbi Morrison is frequently featured in the Torah section of the Arutz Sheva website, and his work can be read on his own website at http://ravkooktorah.org. His first book of essays of Rav Kook's writings, *Gold from the Land of Israel*, was published by Urim Publications in 2006.